D0577036

CALGARY PUBLIC LIBRARY

FEB / - 2016
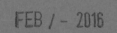

HOW TO BE A
CYCLIST

First published in Great Britain in 2014 by Arena Sport, an imprint of Birlinn Ltd

Birlinn Ltd
West Newington House
10 Newington Road
Edinburgh
EH9 1QS

www.arenasportbooks.co.uk

ISBN 978 1 90971 515 8
eBook ISBN 978 0 85790 803 2

Copyright © John Deering and Phil Ashley, 2014

The right of John Deering and Phil Ashley to be identified as the authors of this work have been asserted by them in accordance with the Copyright, Designs and Patents Act 1988.

All rights reserved. No part of this publication may be reproduced, stored, or transmitted in any form, or by any means electronic, mechanical or photocopying, recording or otherwise, without the express written permission of the publisher.

The authors have made every effort to clear all copyright permissions, but where this has not been possible and amendments are required, the publisher will be pleased to make any necessary arrangements at the earliest opportunity.

British Library Cataloguing-in-Publication Data
A catalogue record for this book is available on request from the British Library.

All photography by philashley.com, and the following contributors: Phil Ashley author picture Dan Tsantilis;
40, 106 John Deering; 164 Mondadori/Getty Images; 165 Doug Pensinger/Getty Images;
167 Procycling Magazine/Getty Images; 220 Emily Ashley.

Layout and Cover design by Jane Ashley
Printed and bound in Latvia

HOW TO BE A
CYCLIST

AN A–Z OF LIFE ON TWO WHEELS

Words by John Deering
Photography by Phil Ashley

John Deering's first book, *Team on the Run*, was a study of his time with the chaotic but charismatic Linda McCartney Cycling Team and went on to be voted fifth best cycling book of all time. He followed that with *Bradley Wiggins: Tour de Force* and he spent much of 2013 working with British cycling legend Sean Yates on his autobiography, *It's all about The Bike*, shortlisted for Cycling Book of the Year. John first worked with Phil Ashley on their acclaimed *12 Months in the Saddle*. He has supplied many features to publications such as *Procycling*, *The Official Tour de France Guide* and *Ride Cycling Review*, and contributed regularly to *Eurosport*'s cycling coverage. Cycling and cycling writing has taken him round the world, but he prefers the mean streets of south west London to anywhere else. He lives in Richmond with his Giant Defy Advanced.

Phil Ashley has followed a life in photography. After studying in Hertfordshire and Swansea, he returned to London to spend his younger years working in the studios of many leading lights of the art. At just 25 he set up his own studio and has spent many of the intervening years photographing people, products and places for the likes of the *Observer*, Nokia, GlaxoSmithKline and Getty Images. Phil's first bike was a Raleigh Record Sprint, to the envy of his schoolfriends. He turned away from cycling in his teens after destroying an unknown family's picnic when taking the wrong route down Box Hill. His conversion to the delights of road cycling in the early part of the twenty-first century is accompanied by an uncommon zeal and he weighs considerably less than he used to. He lives in Middlesex with his wife and daughter.

HOW TO BE A CYCLIST

Welcome, Pilgrim. Enter. Relax. You have travelled far, you who would seek wisdom?

Near Guildford.

Ah, Guildford. Gateway to the provinces. Here, have a coffee. Black coffee. And what do you think you're doing with that sugar?

Oh, sorry. No sugar?

It needs to be earned, Pilgrim. Here endeth the first lesson. No charge for that one.

Well, that's very kind of you I must say, Mr—?

No misters round here. I am The Guide.

OK. Thanks, The Guide, I'm …

I know who you are. You are Pilgrim. But I like your face, son, so I'm going to let you skip the definite article. Now, in your own words, Pilgrim, tell me why you think you're here.

Umm … to get better at cycling?

Right. Well, that will be one of the benefits of coming under my tutelage, but that's a bit like saying that Gareth Bale joined Real Madrid to improve his Spanish. It'll happen, but there is a slightly wider perspective.

Wider?

Indeed, Pilgrim, as broad as the deep blue sea itself. You are here to begin your journey upon the road to knowledge, power and true enlightenment. Invincible health, devastating erudition, unimaginable wealth and prowess with the ladies are all there for the taking, providing you listen to me and follow my instructions with care and deference.

Wow.

Well might you 'Wow', Pilgrim. I'm not fucking about with the little stuff here, son.

The ladies, you say?

Indeed, Pilgrim. One of the things I already know about you is that you're absolutely hopeless at understanding the fairer sex.

That's outrageous. How dare you? I'll have you know that I ... I ... Oh, OK, fair enough. But how did you know that?

Never met a cyclist who did have a clue, to be honest. But we can fix that.

But what about the ladies you see riding bikes?

Pilgrim, do you know what a MAMIL is?

Yes. It's a middle-aged man in Lycra.

That's right, a middle-aged *man* in Lycra. Ladies aren't sad and deluded enough to think that spending the equivalent of a mid-size South American republic's GDP on carbon fibre, Assos and Castelli will make them better people. Women riding bikes just aren't as tragic as you. They go bike riding because it's fun. But for you, Pilgrim – a devotee, an acolyte – it's so much more, isn't it? You want to make cycling your life, don't you?

Yeah, I suppose. What's Assos?

Ah, so much to learn. Listen carefully, Pilgrim, because this is some important shit: I know how you feel. The Guide has love, affection and deep, deep understanding for the MAMIL. I know what it's like to wake up at 3 a.m. in a cold sweat thinking that you've only done 50km this week and it's already Thursday. I know how it feels to believe you look like Eddy Merckx then catch a glimpse of yourself

in a shop window and find out it's a lot more Eddie the Eagle. Yes, Pilgrim, you may well sigh and nod. But, equally, I know what it feels like to sit in the pub waiting for your Sunday roast surrounded by bleary-eyed *Observer* readers who've just rolled out of bed when you've already ridden the Horseshoe Pass that morning. You want that, don't you, Pilgrim?

Yes! Yes, I want that!

But you're scared, aren't you, Pilgrim? Blundering around this arcane world of tubular tyres, Roubaix Lycra and gear ratios. There's a whole new lexicography waiting to trip up the unwary. There are more pitfalls than a bank holiday *Total Wipeout Celebrity Special*. It's like *Dangerous Liaisons* but without a Pfeiffer.

It's just so frightening.

I know, I know, Pilgrim. Take my hand. I shall be your guide. But beware, for the way of the Guide, to paraphrase the King James Bible, is bloody hard. I eschew frippery. I turn my back on big nights out. I say 'No!' to takeaway pizza. Sometimes. I choose a good night's sleep and five hours in the drizzle around Kent instead. I feel your pain and I share your joy, Pilgrim. Are you ready?

Yes! Help me, Guide!

Hmm. Tell you what, I'll see what I can do.

Right: *Hello, are you the Guide? I could do with some guidance.*

Contents

A is for ATTITUDE

Take a deep breath. Fill those lungs. Feel the spring sunshine tickling the four inches of bare shaved skin between the top of your mid-length socks and the bottom of your Swiss Lycra knee warmers. Check your speed on the Garmin. In kilometres, not miles. You are a pro. These are the hours of preparation for the big one. This is the time for you to measure yourself against your rivals. Hold that tummy in. Remember: got to be back by one to pick up the wife's mother.

So, let me ask you a question, Pilgrim: do you ride a bike for money?

Money? Err, no, not for money. For fun, I suppose.

Working upon the premise that if we're not doing something for money then we're doing it for fun, then you are, to a degree, correct. However, there will be many, many seconds, minutes, hours, days and weeks when it is no fun whatsoever.

Forgive the impertinence, Guide, but if it's not for fun, what is it for?

Just because cycling is not your profession, doesn't mean we can't approach it in a professional manner. Be a professional at all times. To answer your question, your goal is something much deeper, much more emphatic than simple fun, Pilgrim. Your hours in the saddle are designed to bring you closer to karma, to true understanding of this world we share. You are here to become a better person. A better word than fun would be enjoyment. Concentrate on a deep, satisfied state of enjoyment, and then, maybe, you can have fun. Because, as you suggested earlier, it is meant to be fun. Eventually.

Oh right. OK then. Where do I start?

Inside yourself, Pilgrim. Inside your head, your heart, your very soul. I am going to prepare you, immerse you in the cooling waters of knowledge. Ready?

Is it cold? Should I have bought a rain jacket?

Oh dear, I can see I'm going to have to be a lot more literal with you. Have you heard of Eros Poli, Pilgrim?

Hmm. Eros … Eros … Anything to do with Piccadilly Circus?

Yeah. No. No, not really. Eros Poli was the six foot four, 85kg Italian *rouleur* who took the most brilliant individual stage win in Tour de France history. OK, there are some great stories about the stars and their exploits, but the key thing about Eros is that he wasn't a star. He was a worker, a *domestique*, a *gregario*. Now, the night of Sunday, 17 July 1994 was a very long one for our Eros, as it was the hottest night of the year, he was marooned in a hotel in the south of France and he still had a week left in the longest, hottest Tour in memory. He'd already spent the best part of 300km in long

breaks, trying to take something home from a race that had been marked by the absence of his leader, Mario Cipollini, through injury. In fact, way back in the seventh stage, he had spent over 100 miles on his own trying to get a win, only to get caught within sniffing distance of the finish.

Gutted.

You'd think so, eh? On this night, it was so hot that his roommate had dragged his duvet out on to the balcony and was sleeping out there. But the heat wasn't the only thing on Eros's mind, Pilgrim: it was the World Cup final that night.

Oh yeah! 1994. That was California, Brazil versus Italy, wasn't it?

It was. The time difference meant that the game went on late into the French night; and extra time and penalties didn't help.

Above: A cycling cap older than your teeth. Respect.

Right: The grim winter miles will all be worthwhile when you finally feel that sunshine on your white calves.

Jesus, how must he have felt when Baggio put his penalty over the bar?

I think we're back with gutted. Want to know what Eros did? He got up a couple of hours later, drank a lot of coffee, then went on a lone break again. Not any old break, either. It was 231km over Mont Ventoux, one of the most feared mountains in cycling, and it was about 40 degrees.

Wait a second. Ventoux? Didn't you say he was six foot four and 85kg? That's the size of two Marco Pantanis. How did he do it?

By riding so hard to get to the foot of the climb that he was twenty minutes in front.

My God. How far in front was he at the top?

Four minutes, with 40km left to go. No bother for our boy. But what I want to tell you about Eros is his advice for you when you're trying to overcome the odds and they're stacked against you, when you're sweating, grunting, trying and failing to conquer a huge mountain that stands between you and reaching your goal.

I'm listening. What does Eros say?

He says: this is a beautiful place. You're not sitting behind a desk. Enjoy yourself.

That's some attitude.

The Guide agrees with you, Pilgrim. Come with me and we shall follow the path of Eros. Actually, on second thoughts, that sounds a bit weird. Let's just get on with it. Let's start with a checklist to make sure you are correctly prepared.

Go for it, Guide.

Left: *Box Hill. Piccadilly Circus for cyclists.*

Always wear a helmet. Eros may have preferred the wind in his hair, but that was the nineties. It's the twenty-first century, and you have to wear one if you're a pro.

Is it acceptable to wear a cap?

A cycling cap is a good thing to carry; you can put it under your lid if it's pouring with rain, or stick it on at the café. Riding wearing a cap instead of a helmet is really only an option if you live in the thirties or you're one of those Shoreditch types who waxes his moustache.

Got it. Anything else I need to know about lids?

Yes. The most important thing. Mountain bike helmets have peaks; road bike helmets do not. Take that peak off and discard it immediately. This is one of the things that will immediately differentiate the pro from the IDWID.

I'm sorry, did you say 'idwid'?

Yes. An acronym for I dunno what I'm doing. Peak on the helmet: you must be an IDWID. Bike upside down for any, *any*, reason: you must be an IDWID.

Aren't they easier to fix upside down?

Oh yeah, much easier. That's why all garages turn cars over before they start work on them. Anyway, that's enough about IDWIDs for now. Let's get this helmet right. It needs to be parallel on your head, not on the back of your bonce. If there's no mirror handy, look up: you should just be able to see the front of it. That's why you don't want a peak. If you've got your lid on properly and your position on the bike is correct, a peak will stop you seeing where you're going.

Sorted. Thanks, Guide.

Are you ready, Pilgrim?

As I'll ever be.

Right: *The Koppenberg can reduce even the best to walking. So this lot have no chance.*

Below: *Lord of all you survey.*

B is for BIKE

In the old days, all the frames were made of steel. They were cheap. Different alloys of steel, of chromium and molybdenum, the Dark Ages really. Then the hard, light, stiff aluminium bikes started arriving: first from America, then Italy and Taiwan. Before long, the directional carbon fibre weaves the manufacturers used for forks to take the sting out of the aluminium were being glued together to make whole frames. The Americans started drawing titanium tubes to tune the ride again. The Taiwanese started making complete moulds for monocoque carbon frames. Over in Europe, the cutting-edge manufacturers found a new material that had outrageous capabilities for bike building: it was strong, light, stiff and absorbent, and could be shaped into a frame custom-tuned for you. It was amazingly expensive. It was called steel.

Right then, Pilgrim, let's talk about bikes. Let's talk about bikes, baby. Let's talk about you and me. Let's talk about all the good things and the bad things that may be.

Bikes! Brilliant, yes! That's what I'm here for!

Woah, hold your horses there, boy. You're not here for bikes, you're here for cycling. An easy mistake to make, granted, but a mistake nonetheless. We all know somebody who talks about compact versus traditional, Campag versus Shimano, steel versus aluminium, Selle Italia versus San Marco, and who hasn't been on a bike since they were ridden in black

and white. Don't be that man, Pilgrim. The bike is merely the chassis; you are the engine. It's you we're here for, not the wheels.

Fair enough. I do like bikes though.

And well you might. Good, aren't they? Let's go through a few things.

I'm all ears.

First of all, let's talk about what bikes are made of, or to be more specific, what bike frames are made of. The bare minimum you need to get you going is a decent

aluminium frame. Yes, that's al-you-min-ee-um, not aloominum. Tell any Americans you pass on the road that there are two I's in the word. Now, aluminium is great stuff for making bikes. It's light, it's stiff, it's strong, it's relatively easy to work with, so it makes for a lively, responsive, nippy, inexpensive ride. Unfortunately, the other thing aluminium is really good at is transmitting shock. To combat that, you need to have a carbon fibre fork to soak up a bit of road buzz. That's a prerequisite.

Got it: aluminium frames need a carbon fork.

Good. Now, whole frames made out of carbon have been available for about 25 years, but it's only in the past decade that they've reached maturity.

Why's that? You'd think that if you could make a fork out of the stuff, then a frame would be straightforward.

Two things, really. The first is a matter of understanding the forces that a frame is subjected to. Carbon fibre sheets are directional, so they're ideal for forks. You can make it laterally very stiff to make the handling true and predictable, but absorbent perpendicularly, to take the sting out of rough roads. Frames are much more complicated; there's a lot more going on. You need the back end to be stiff to give you value for the effort you're putting in, you need the front end not to twist when you're pounding the pedal on one side and pulling on the opposing side of the handlebars, but you want the whole thing to be light and absorbent too. It's taken them a while to figure that out.

I see. What's the other thing?

How you put the thing together. The first carbon frames were tubes, glued into lugs, not that different to welded metal frames. In fact, the lugs were metal on the older ones. The benefit was that they were

Left: *Take your pick. They're all good.*

TCR
3 ISP ... ED SL

FRAME
Advanced SL-Grade Co...

FORK
Advanced SL-Grade Composite, ... Seatpost
OverDrive 2 Steerer

SHIFTERS
Shimano Ultegra 22 speed

BRAKES
Shimano Ultegra

COLOURS
White/Silver

SIZES
S, M, M/L, L

£2,999

ON ROAD | PERFORMANCE | Race

easy to make and you could tune the size easily by cutting the tubes to length, but they were relatively heavy and a lot of the absorbency was lost with all those joints. These days, the ultimate is to have what they call a monocoque frame, where a mould is made for the whole thing. That's financially prohibitive though, so there's a balancing act between cost and delivery. The best off-the-peg bikes are usually two or three pieces put together.

You can get really cheap carbon frames now, can't you?

Yes, but be careful. Not all carbon is the same. There are as many different types as there are metals. You can spend a grand on a carbon bike, or three grand on a frame alone. Logic should tell you they're not the same thing.

OK. Buyer beware. Are all the professionals riding carbon?

The vast majority, but that doesn't necessarily mean they're the best bikes. Bike manufacturers put a lot of cash into teams and they expect them to ride the things they're trying to sell, and that, largely, means carbon fibre bikes.

What else is there?

Well, one of the drawbacks of carbon fibre frames is the difficulty in providing a made-to-measure bike because a mould is so expensive. Titanium has been the dream material for a long time, but it's now found a niche as the ideal stuff for making custom frames out of. Ti bikes, like carbon ones, chase the Holy Grail combination of low weight, stiffness, comfort and strength.

Left: *Ain't about the cha-ching, ain't about the ba-bling, forget about the price tag.*

Right: *Carbon fibre won't rust.*

The trouble is, they cost loads; but if you want a custom fit, it's straightforward to weld one to your shape, rather than knocking up an expensive mould. The other advantage of ti is that it doesn't deteriorate. It ought to be the same in twenty years' time, providing you don't ride it into a brick wall.

Were you saying something about steel earlier?

Ah, the old favourite. If you want a bit of class, a bit of personality, it's hard to beat. And they've got better at it. The best steel is light and stiff, and it's always been the most comfortable ride. But the real joy is in the personal touch. The relationship between builder and rider is a beautiful thing.

I like the idea of having something with a bit of history behind it.

Remember this: good steel or aluminium bikes come from Europe. Mainly England and Italy. The best carbon comes out of Taiwan. Some people get upset when they hear that their prestigious Italian marque carbon fibre bike was actually fabricated in the Far East, but they're wrong. The carbon bike industry in Europe is nascent to say the least. It's a good thing that it's made out there. As for titanium, the Americans rock.

So much to think about, Guide.

Sweet dreams, Pilgrim.

Left: *You don't need to own all the right tools. You need to know somebody who does, though.*

Overleaf: *The Weald from Firle Beacon, a high spot of the South Downs ridge.*

is for CAFÉ

Please, don't let us stop at the café at the top of the hill today.

Now then, Pilgrim, let us discuss the trials and tribulations of café culture. The dos and don'ts. The opportunities and the pitfalls.

I love cafés, me. You can't beat a bacon butty, can you?

Oh dear, oh dear, oh dear. Pilgrim, what are we going to do with you?

What?

I was hoping that incident with the coffee might have given you some kind of grounding.

I can only drink black coffee without sugar?

Before a ride or when you're not riding, that is correct, Pilgrim. But, on the post-ride stop, you can treat yourself to a cappuccino. You can even sprinkle a bit of chocolate on it. Fuck it, scatter three grains of brown sugar on the foam; you've earned it.

Can I have that bacon butty now?

No! There is never a time that is cool for the bacon butty. It goes like this: first, eat some porridge or muesli at home before you leave. That's the best preparation for a few hours' riding. If you're meeting in the café before the ride, you may have an espresso. If you've got to wait for a bit, then an americano is acceptable. If you really can't abide the idea of coffee without milk, then I will allow you a macchiato while you're weaning yourself off it.

What can I eat in the café after the ride then?

Cake is very popular. The legendary Sean Yates, close personal friend of the Guide, used to rate the type of cake and the size of slice dependent on the length and intensity of the ride. Thus, a spin round the lanes on a Sunday morning will buy you a skinny blueberry muffin, whereas a six-hour hilly ride could yield a massive chunk of Black Forest gâteau.

It's all so confusing. What if we stop halfway round?

Ooh, the dangers of the halfway stop.

Don't tell me: pitfalls?

Rife. Rife with pitfalls, the halfway stop. The biggest danger is the onset of the crippling condition known to the medical profession as 'café legs'.

That sounds bad.

Reminds me of Kevin Keegan's oft-repeated assertion that cramp can be worse than a broken leg. If your café stop is at the bottom of a hill — they often seem to be — then the first mile or two after you leave will be replete with agonising pain shooting through your calves and thighs. If your café stop is at the top of a hill — the ones that aren't at the bottom always seem to be — then you will be plagued with chills that will do their best to shiver you out of the saddle before you get to the bottom.

Right: *It's about time you did a turn on the front, Pilgrim.*

So what's your advice, Guide?

Don't stop until you'll nearly home. Café legs are funny when you're just round the corner, but much less amusing when you've got a couple of hours to go.

Can I sit inside?

Ah, good question, Pilgrim, you're concentrating. Let's just roll things back for a moment. Before you choose your table, you need to successfully park your bicycle, am I right? This is another opportunity to spot the IDWID.

I'm listening.

Good lad. Now, this is important. Whenever you lean your bike up against something, make sure the back tyre is against it: wall, tree, lamppost, whatever. If the bike tyre is touching it, it won't roll away and is thus much less likely to fall over.

Ooh, good one, Guide.

C'est rien, mon ami. Take off your helmet. Refasten the strap. Hang it from the rear end of your handlebar stem so that the lid hangs between the bars, the top side facing the road ahead. This is how the pros do it. You may now remove that cap from your jersey pocket where it has been attracting moisture, and place it on your head. The peak always points down, no matter how many PG Tips adverts you've seen.

Can you ride tandem?

Exactly. Now, if you are with a friend, he may carefully lie his bike against yours, as long as it is essentially upright and only touching yours to avoid falling over. Leaning is bad. Also, his bike should face in the opposing direction, and any subsequent bikes should also be top to toe, thus taking up the least possible

Left: *Hardy adventurers face the threat of café legs head on.*

amount of space. Never, ever, lay your bike on the ground. This is golden IDWID territory. If, through some convoluted series of events you find yourself in a barren land and in need of a pee with nothing to lean your bike on, lean it on your own backside as you bend forward to fish in your bib shorts. If you have somehow become an IDWID and lain your trusty steed on the dirt – I can think of no extenuating circumstances that would permit this – don't for one moment lay it gear-side-down. That's firing squad time.

So can I go inside?

Ah yes, the inside conundrum. Let us first assume that you are not carrying a lock. You're bike riding, not shopping at Iceland. If you are unable to see the bike from the indoor table, then, no, you can't go in.

If you can see it, but it's at a distance, remove your carefully handlebar-hung helmet and refasten it to join your front wheel to the frame. That ought to stop the opportunist. It's not cool, but it's cooler than walking home wondering what happened to your bike.

Wise words, Guide.

Hey, don't thank me, Pilgrim. This is my job.

Above: *No more than three grains of brown sugar can be added.*

Right: *This is a three-hour-ride slice of cake.*

D is for DRUGS

Bloody disgrace. Chargers. Ruining our sport, the sport we love.

It used to be about chivalry, bravery, the refusal to give in to the body's weakness.

Coppi, Anquetil, Simpson, Merckx, Pantani. They were the greats.

They would never have taken drugs. Have you got the Voltarol, Dave?

So, Pilgrim, has anybody asked you about drugs yet?

Drugs? I'm not planning on doing that. Is that what you meant when you said I had to be professional?

No, no, no, of course not. Calm yourself. I bring the subject up because people you meet in social situations will doubtless seek to denigrate your sport with the wearying supposition that it is terminally undermined by the history of drug abuse that has stained its many achievements. They'll scoff at your chosen calling by suggesting that everybody knows that anybody who has ever turned a pedal in anger is a cheat.

Emm, I don't quite know how to ask this ... but, is it ... is cycling ...

Spit it out, Pilgrim. We're all friends here.

Does everybody in cycling take drugs?

There are plenty who will tell you yes, but they, Pilgrim, are the uninformed. There have always been cyclists who didn't take drugs, and the sport is cleaner now than at any time. Testing is better, the authorities actually want to catch the cheats, which hasn't always been the case, and the way the top guys

train and race has improved no end. The secret is in the numbers, you see, Pilgrim.

No, I don't see. What numbers?

The riders at the top all know how much power they can put out and what is sustainable. They also know this information, roughly, about their opponents. So, if you're Chris Froome and you're knocking out, say, 500 watts on Mont Ventoux and Vincenzo Nibali attacks you, you can confidently stick to your plan in the knowledge that his burst will be short-lived. In the bad old days of EPO and its derivatives, you wouldn't be able to trust your opponents. If somebody attacked like that, you might never see him again.

Ah, OK, now I do see. So the results are real now?

The Guide will stick his neck out and say yes, they are. If Bradley Wiggins ever comes up on a doping charge for his 2012 win, I'll eat my Condor

cap. Because that's the other thing: retrospective stripping of titles is very popular these days. Just ask Lance Armstrong.

Ah, Lance. Is he pure evil, then?

You can make a case for him being the biggest cheat of all time. He won more Tours than anyone else and he cheated to do it, QED. However, there's a huge amount of hypocrisy tangled up in the vilification of Armstrong. You'd have to be able to go back and retest everybody that won a bike race in the nineties, eighties, seventies, sixties, fifties, forties . . . in fact, back to when the bike was invented. It certainly leaves the Guide scratching his prodigiously endowed head that Armstrong is publicly excoriated while Marco Pantani, known and punished doper who died from a drug overdose, is revered and idolised to the extent that he had an official tribute paid to him in the 2013 Giro d'Italia. The Giro was a race that he'd tried to win by cheating.

So I don't need drugs?

Not that type, Pilgrim. But there are plenty of legal substances designed to make you unbeatable.

You mean like gels, energy drinks, that sort of stuff?

Left: *The narrow lanes of the Surrey Hills could be a thousand miles from suburban London.*

Above: *The wind-blasted upper slopes of Ventoux are hallowed ground for any cyclist.*

I sure do. But take care with that shit, Pilgrim, unless you have a copper-lined stomach. The racing professional's musette is not full of all that rubbish like they'd have you believe. It's more likely to feature the delights of the cheese and jam roll, jelly beans and a can of Coke.

Really? But bike shops sell heaps and heaps of that stuff!

Yes, they do, and it has its place. Take the energy gel, for instance. You should always carry one with you. And that's what you should do with it: carry it, deep in a jersey pocket where it will snuggle for many rides, far, far beyond its sell-by date. That energy gel is your get out of jail free card, what you need to get you out of the hole you should never have fallen into.

You don't eat them all the time, then?

Christ, no. Your gut will rot quicker than George Best's if you follow the manic idiom of three gels an hour. That's fifteen on a reasonable ride. Good grief. The gel is there to give you a quick hit, and it does it very well, but there is a corresponding dip. If you're an hour from home and stuck to the road because you haven't eaten properly, or it's all been a

Mungrisdale is in the lesser-trodden folds of Cumbria, and none the worse for it.

bit beyond you, get that gel out. Beware: if you take it earlier, you'll be gulping them for the rest of the day. The man who swallows an energy gel in the morning is an amateur indeed; it might give him a quick hit, but there'll be hell to pay with the corresponding dip. And the stomach swirling with sugary gloop.

What about energy bars?

They're not a bad idea at all. Get one that you like to eat, that isn't too unnatural, and take a bite every twenty minutes or so on a long ride. It won't give you an amphetamine-like boost like they claim a gel can –

you'd have to be totally fucked in the first place for it to work like that – but it will keep your levels topped up and help you maintain an even keel.

Drinks?

Water is still great at hydrating. Funny, that. Though a carb drink can help, as long as you haven't mixed it too strong. What tastes all right in the kitchen can taste like golden syrup after a couple of hours in the saddle. There are also those zero calorie tablets you can drop into water, like a Berocca. If they persuade you to drink more because they taste nicer than

water, then do it. You can't overdo it. And if you have trouble digesting it on the go, don't forget to take a big slug whenever you stop. It all goes down the same way. If you've got two bottle cages – you will have, because pros have two cages – make sure the bottles you use match, then have water in one and energy drink in the other. Simples. Oh, and keep your empty bottles in the freezer. It sterilises them and lessens the great flavour of plastic.

Top tip, thanks.

You're welcome. Another tip on the theme of bottles is to do with the cages they ride in. Carbon ones look nice and flash, but for bumpy roads and cobbles you can't beat a good old-fashioned, lightweight aluminium cage, as you can bend them for a tighter fit. You see bottles rolling all round Flanders when you go over there for a sportive, thanks to the ubiquitous carbon fibre. And one last pro touch: don't call them bottles, call them bidons.

Why?

Because I say so. And finally, Pilgrim, please remember that energy food lives in jersey pockets. Never in a little box-shaped bag on your top tube. And never, *ever*, taped to that same tube in a line with four or five others of varying unnatural flavours. Have a little dignity.

Left: *Go steady on the Go gels.*

Below: *Nothing can bring back the hour of splendour in the grass.*

Overleaf: *The winding, dipping, silent roads of the Northwest Highlands are closely guarded secrets for those in the know.*

E is for ETIQUETTE

Is it too much to ask? When I slowly nod my head or raise a finger from my bars as I pass you going the other way, stranger, could you return a similar gesture? Just a slight inclination of the brow or the suggestion of a half-smile. It's all I ask. We're all in this together, brother. No, not you, mountain biker. No, not you, commuter. You, comrade road cyclist. You, tribal brother. Or are you a triathlete? Sorry, my mistake.

Club culture is dying, Pilgrim.

I'm not so sure. I still see a long line of kids without coats on queuing for Dusk in Guildford on Saturday nights. I think that's the one where Cheryl Cole belted the lady in the toilets, but they've changed the name now.

Not that type of club culture. Cycling club culture, you fool.

Of course, sorry. And it might not have been that one anyway, there's two or three.

Look at me. I'm ignoring you. Right. In the old days, you had to be in a cycling club. You just had to. You had to be in one if you wanted to race, effectively. OK, there were ways round it, but the whole thing was secretive and mysterious. That was because racing on the road was illegal in the UK for most of the bicycle's existence, and even when it was legalised, the participants found it best to sneak around in black jackets and give the courses codenames. The E72, for goodness sake. It's already got a codename: the A12. How many codenames does a road need?

It's different now though?

Very much so. I'd say it started with organisations like the Surrey League.

I've heard of that. What is it?

Good, Pilgrim, well done. The Surrey League, and others like it, was set up to make it easier to race. You could just pitch up. They sought out closed roads like motor racing circuits, aerodromes and MOD facilities, so there wouldn't be any conflict with other road users. Then the national federation cottoned on and introduced a new category, 4th Cat, so you could ride against other people who didn't know what they were doing either. It was a great testing ground, and if you managed to get your wings and move up to 3rd Cat, you'd be accomplished enough by then not to piss off the blokes who were already there.

So it opened the sport up? Sounds like a great thing.

Yes, it was. The clubs were intimidating for newcomers; they all had their very peculiar ways of doing things that they didn't realise were peculiar. There was a lot of 'Point of order, Mr Chairman' type stuff going on, and committees. Oh, the committees. Some clubs had more committees than members.

Great stuff all round. Everybody's happy now, then.

Well, not quite. You see, the clubs were fantastic places to learn how to ride a bike. I'm not talking about when your dad takes your stabilisers off, I'm talking about the stuff you need to know to ride properly. How to sit right. How to pedal nicely. How to go round corners. How to stay out of the wind. How to ride in a bunch.

And that's all useful stuff that people need to know.

You're not wrong, Pilgrim. The better clubs have modernised, and membership is booming, but it's not

Left: *Learn how to go round a corner on your own before you subject others to your idiosyncrasies.*

keeping pace with the number of new cyclists. There are more people cycling, and there are more people in cycling clubs, but the proportion of people cycling who are not in clubs is bigger than ever. If you look at the skill of the average cyclist, it's dropped as the sport has grown. Where that gap is most keenly felt though, is in the erosion of etiquette: how to deal with other cyclists on the road.

Should I say hello to everybody?

As a rule, yes. I suppose there must be a tipping point, a critical mass where it is no longer practical. I mean, if you had a car in Edwardian times, you'd probably have waved at other car drivers. You'd look a bit of a cock trying to greet everybody coming the other way on the M6 these days. If you're riding to work, say, on one of Boris's blue superhighways, there is unlikely to be much time to converse with your fellow wage

monkeys. If, however, you are trundling around the lanes at the weekend and you see a like-minded fellow passing the other way, it still feels grossly impolite to the Guide if you don't acknowledge each other's presence in some way.

What if you're going the same way as somebody?

Ah, a much more complicated kettle of halibut, Pilgrim. First, the onus is on the pursuer to greet the captured soul. If you're heading straight by, a simple 'Morning' will suffice. But consider this: perhaps you're travelling at a similar velocity, you've only been brought together very slowly, or by a junction causing you both to await a gap in the traffic.

Below: *The backmarker is forced to dismount in shame after committing a heinous sock crime.*

Right: *Are you half wheeling me again?*

I could just sit on his wheel.

You disappoint me, Pilgrim. First, you must decide if you want company. If not, and you judge yourself able, accelerate gently without obviously doing so and resort to the 'Morning' mentioned above as you set about putting a seemly gap between you and your short-lived companion. If you fancy someone to talk to, ask him politely where he's from, how far he's going. From the way he answers you, you'll probably get a fair idea of whether he's amenable to a bit of company or whether he's likely to jam a screwdriver between your gums at the first available opportunity. At this point, if you want to continue with him, ask his permission. It would be a cruel man to refuse you, but a rude one who didn't ask.

What if it's a bunch of guys?

Similar story. Say hello, ask permission if you want to ride with them. In the old days, if you didn't have mudguards on – pros do not use mudguards – you would only be allowed to ride with a bunch if you stayed at the back.

A big club came past me the other day and not one of them said hello.

Yeah, I bet I know who they were. Wankers. Don't worry about it. Take the moral high ground.

So what about all that other stuff they used to teach you in cycling clubs?

What do you think you've got the Guide for? Stick with me, kid. I'm coming to that.

Left: *Bikes don't have to be new to be flash.*

Right: *If you wait for me at the top, I'll tell you what you've been doing wrong.*

F is for Fit

I, also, am a massive fan of Charlie Chaplin's films. His earlier work is of the highest comedic quality, while the latter part of his canon runs over with moving pathos. His career-long exploration of the timeless theme of little man versus big man never runs dry and has withstood the test of a century passing. However, unlike you, I don't feel the need to pay homage to the great man by riding everywhere with my knees sticking out at right angles like that. Or have you just borrowed that bike off the butcher's boy?

Would you buy a suit without trying it on, Pilgrim?

Never!

Would you spend upwards of three grand on one, perhaps, without it fitting?

Never!

Then why do people do that with bikes all the time? It's baffling. Before we go any further with the details, take on board this one salient fact and have it ready at all times: the cheap bike that fits you will always beat the expensive one that doesn't. Got it, Pilgrim?

The cheap bike that fits you will always beat the expensive one that doesn't. Got it.

Good lad.

Does that mean I need a custom-built frame?

No. The decent manufacturers do a good range of sizes now, and the better shops will soon tell you if one maker's geometry doesn't really suit you. You need to get the frame size right, yes, but most of the optimisation comes through how you set the bike up.

Handlebar width, crank length, that sort of thing?

You've been reading up, Pilgrim — well done — but we're coming at this from the wrong end. We need to concentrate on you, the rider, and then the pieces of the jigsaw will fall into place.

OK. It's all about me.

We're making a triangle of feet, bum and hands. That triangle is unique to you. You can tweak it a little bit depending on things like your weight, type of riding and flexibility, but essentially that perfect triangle is what we're trying to find.

How do we do that, Guide?

The easiest way is to get measured by somebody who knows what they're doing. Give your local bike shop a test. If you point out a bike they've got on the shop floor and they ask you to sit on it and, hey presto, the guy tells you it's the perfect size for you, you are either genuinely the luckiest man alive or, more than likely, about to get properly striped up. Yes, it's a good idea to have an idea of the bike you want before you get measured — you don't get measured for a jacket when you're buying trousers, after all — but measuring should be a little bit more scientific than a salesman saying 'Perfect!'

So what do we need to know? Saddle height?

That's probably the single most important one, but also the easiest to sort. You can easily move a seat post up and down but you can't wind handlebars in or out. But while we're at it, let's talk about what

Right: *Half an hour on a fitting jig will be the most useful 30 minutes you ever spend on a bike.*

constitutes a good saddle height. You might need a willing minion with you when you're doing this. Take your shoes off and sit squarely on the saddle. Roll the pedals round until one is at the bottom of the revolution, then rest your heel on it.

My heel? Not the ball of my foot?

No, your leg should be comfortably straight when your heel rests on the pedal when it's at its lowest point. Get that minion to stand behind you and make sure you're not dropping your hip to reach for it. You do it with your heel so that your knee will be gently bent when the ball of your foot is over the pedal axle. When you're happy, measure from the centre of the cranks up the seat tube to the top of your saddle and make a note of it. If you always use that measurement as a starting point, you won't be far off it. Are you still with me, Pilgrim?

Yes. What next?

The other point of the triangle is more awkward. It's really best to see an expert. The reach is essential but tricky to get right.

I heard something about putting your elbow against the front of the saddle and touching the handlebar stem with the tips of your fingers.

Yes, I've heard that too. Bollocks, I'm afraid, Pilgrim. It doesn't allow for the length of that stem — it's the distance to the bars that's important, not to the stem — and you need to have your saddle the right distance behind the cranks, otherwise you'll just be pushing up and down instead of pedalling nice reliable circles. Nice idea, but meaningless.

Left: *The mossy depths of Borrowdale lead to the killer passes of central Lakeland.*

So what is the position I'm trying to achieve?

You want your hands to sit relaxed on top of your levers with your weight equally shared between feet, bum and hands. This is your number one position, so you want this to be the one you consider the most carefully. How high your bars are in relation to your saddle depends on your flexibility more than anything else. Having a higher front end and a shorter reach is often referred to, a touch euphemistically, as the sportive position. I'm not convinced that this position

is any better for riding sportives than it is for racing; it's just that the man riding a sportive may be, let's just say, a little less bendy than his racing counterpart. And there's often something else in between him and his bike.

What's that?

His gut.

Oh, I see. So upright positions are for fatties?

I wouldn't go that far. There are a lot of people with lower back issues, neck problems and so on who benefit from a higher and nearer front end. But you don't want to end up looking like those Americans who have head tubes longer than seat tubes, and whose position has more in common with a man pointing a remote control at *America's Next Top Model* than bike riding. I know a shop that offers a free pipe and slippers with every one of those bikes.

So there's no great shortcut for getting this right? I should go and pay somebody to measure me?

If you're buying a bike from a good shop, they'll do it as a matter of course. But, yes, get measured. Unless . . . there is one thing you could do.

Yes, Guide? What's that?

Find an old picture of Roger De Vlaeminck. Stick it to your bedroom mirror. Put your bike alongside it and sit on it until you get it *juuust* right.

Right: *Seriously, do this bit before you buy one.*

Left: *Nice fit. Did you borrow that bike off your dad, son?*

Overleaf: *The man who is tired of Tuscany is tired of cycling.*

G is for Gears

The innovative American bicycle manufacturer Cannondale used to make a single-speed model called the IFG. As it became more popular and people started to ask what the letters stood for, the Cannondale marketing people came out with some guff about tech spec, but the people behind the bike smirked to themselves. They knew what IFG had stood for all along: One Fucking Gear. Nice story, but we'd prefer a few more gears than that where we're headed.

So, Pilgrim. Gears.

I need them, don't I?

You sure do – if you're going to be a pro. Even Eddy Merckx needed gears. Even Lance at his most assisted. Even Pantani used little gears to ride up mountains. Gears are great. Do you want to hear a brief twenty-first-century history of gears?

Yes, please, Guide.

I'm not entirely sure of the truthfulness of that answer, but I appreciate the sentiment.

Tell me anyway.

Don't worry, Pilgrim, I'm going to. In the old days, everybody rode with a 52-tooth outer chain ring and a 42 on the inside. If you're old enough to have ridden bikes like this, you'll probably say 52-'tuth'.

Tuth?

Tuth. To rhyme with, emm, actually, to rhyme with nothing that I can think of. Except 'woof' with a 'th' on the end.

Don't worry, I've got it. Tuth. But people say 'tooth' now?
Or teeth?

Teeth would make more sense, being the plural, but,
yes, people say 'tooth'.

So, old bikes had two chain rings, with 52- and 42-tooth
chain rings?

Right. Those old bikes had five or, if you were lucky,
six cogs at the back, so to get a decent spread of
gears you would need to slip the chain between
the two front rings quite often. Therefore the gap
between them couldn't be too mahoosive, otherwise
you'd lose your pedalling rhythm all the time.

But that's not the case now?

By the nineties, the invention of the quite marvellous
cassette hub meant you could have more gears, and
the rear set went to seven, then eight, then nine . .
. until the current smug ten or even eleven. Some
bright spark, realising that this had doubled the
number of options we had in ye olden days, surmised
that we wouldn't need to change between the front
rings so often, so we could have a bigger gap between
them, use the big one for most riding, and use the
little one for climbing. Hence 'compact' chain sets.

Ah, so that's the compact chain set I've heard about.

Yes, the glorious compact. They shrunk the smallest
of the little cogs at the back too, so you could have
a smaller big ring of, say, 50 teeth, and still spin a gear
out at 35mph. Genius. Nowadays, you can choose
between compact (normally 50-34) and race (53-39).

Left: *There's no such thing as the wrong weather.*

Should I have one?

Honestly, Pilgrim? Yes. Only pros and poseurs need buy the race-style chain set. Compact is the way forward or, more accurately, the way to get up hills.

So I have 50-34 on the front. What about the back?

The first thing about your rear cassette is that you shouldn't worry about whether it's 10- or 11-speed. It's not important. You'll have the same top and bottom gear, you'll just miss one in the middle somewhere.

And that's not important?

Not really, no. The smallest gap you can have between rings on that cassette is, naturally, one tooth. And the smallest cog you can have has eleven teeth on it. Following that logic, the most hardcore 10-speed cassette you can have will be 11-20. In reality, to give yourself a bit of leeway, you start to leave a two-tooth gap between cogs after you get to a certain point. The most common cassette these days will probably be 12-25. The ten cogs will be 12, 13, 14, 15, 16, 17, 19, 21, 23, 25. Bored yet?

Below: *Taking your cassette apart and cleaning it. Beats working, eh?*

Right: *Wipe your chain off and plop a drop of oil on it after every wet ride.*

Actually, I find it embarrassingly fascinating.

Ah, Pilgrim, you are a true disciple. The 12-25 does most folk, or maybe an 11-25, losing the 16, will give you a bit more oomph in a tailwind finishing sprint at the Wobbly Wheelers Open Road Race. If you're looking at the course of one of the more challenging sportive events, you might decide a 12-28 could be better for longer or steeper mountains. And if you're really daunted by Alpe d'Huez, the Angliru or maybe Hardknott Pass, then there is such a cassette as 12-30. Beyond 30 teeth, your derailleur will struggle to cope, so let's just say for the sake of argument that's as far as you can go.

Is it uncool to have a cassette with a 30-tooth bottom gear on it?

That is another good question, Pilgrim. I would say that it's not the height of desirability, but it's a hell of a lot cooler than getting off and walking. So let's just call it horses for courses. There's nothing wrong with changing cassettes depending on where you're headed.

Or having more than one pair of wheels.

You read my mind. Race wheels. Sportive wheels. Training wheels. Winter wheels. Last wheels and testament. You can have a different cassette on all of them.

This could all end up costing me a fortune, couldn't it?

Are you honestly expecting an answer to that, Pilgrim?

Left: *Some roads just beg you to point your bike downhill and whoop.*

Right: *A 28 for getting up there and an 11 to come back down.*

H is for HILLS

There are no great flat bike rides. The hill is your friend. The mountain is your friend. But beware, for the hill is a fickle mistress, guiding you onto the rocks of despair with her beckoning painted fingernail and a toss of her lustrous locks. First one to get off and walk is a wanker.

Climbers are all tiny guys, right, Guide?

That's a truism you often hear, Pilgrim, but it's only partially correct. The real angels of the mountains have always been little fellows: Charly Gaul of Luxembourg was the original bearer of that sobriquet; then there was the mercurial Scot, Robert Millar, eight stone wringing wet; and of course there was the last man to land the Giro/Tour double, the late great Marco Pantani. But weighing as much as a box of Rice Krispies isn't a prerequisite to talent on the slopes.

There are good climbers who aren't little fellers?

Miguel Indurain was a big lad and he destroyed five Tour de France fields from the front in the mountains, shedding riders like drops of water splashed from puddles as he pounded onwards and upwards. Eros Poli was the biggest man in the race, yet he won a Tour stage over Ventoux. Lance Armstrong's Tour successes may have had their roots in the 10kg he left behind when he recovered from cancer, but he was no Mr Puniverse. The key is neither weight nor power; it's power to weight. How much power you need to put out to move your weight up the hill. Do you know who Dr Ferrari is?

Lance's drugs advisor?

Good, Pilgrim. However, it is also grudgingly accepted that he was the man who quantified what we already knew about power to weight. Ferrari came up with the magic number: 6.7. Ignore what Douglas Adams said about the number 42, the real answer to Life, the Universe and Everything is 6.7. According to Ferrari, if you can put out 6.7 watts for every kilogramme of weight you carry, you can win the Tour de France. Mind you, you'll probably have to get your body fat down to about 3% for that.

So Victoria Beckham could win the Tour?

More chance than you, Pilgrim. Hey, come on, don't look so down. Look, it's about what works best for you. Let's assume that you've got your weight down as far as you're likely to without making yourself truly miserable. If you want to order a Domino's Two-for-Tuesday even when your flatmate is out, go for it.

I don't have to starve myself?

The less you weigh, the faster you'll climb. Once we've accepted that, we can move on. Let's think about the type of hill you're facing. For shorter rises, momentum is everything. If you come haring down into a dip and see the road rearing up in front of you, make a quick assessment: is it going to be short enough to blast up the either side? That would be ideal. By barrelling through the bottom, getting out of the saddle and using your rolling speed to power up over the rise, you'll do it quickly and with only the expenditure of a quick burst of energy. You can breathe when you've got up there and can sit down again.

Phew.

Precisely. On the other hand, if you run out of energy halfway up the other side of that dip, it won't be pretty. You'll come to the peak of your trajectory like a cannonball fired straight up into the sky. You'll be weaving across the road like a bluebottle with its feet in tar, and breathing like a goldfish on the kitchen floor.

So it's about judging my effort?

Succinctly put, Pilgrim. On the longer hills, this equation won't come into play. It's just going to be horrible from the bottom to the top, so you might as well get ready for it. The best thing to do is stay sitting, pick a gear that you can roll over at a steady rate and make the best of it. Concentrate on keeping your body still. Every action has an opposite reaction, as my science teacher once told me shortly after he'd caught me pissing in a petri dish and punched me in the ear. If your body is weaving from side to side or your head's nodding like a Churchill Insurance dog, you're wasting energy. This is the time to 'engage your core' as the irritatingly knowledgeable personal trainer will tell you. She's right, of course. Your stomach muscles have a huge part to play in driving you uphill in the seated position, so if you are going to get sucked into any kind of off-bike strengthening or training, core strength improvement will make the biggest difference to your climbing prowess.

Sitting down works better?

For most people on a long climb, yes. Save standing on the pedals for short bursts to give the other muscles a break. Or when there's a photographer at the side of the road. Remember this when you're gasping for air on the upper slopes of the Tourmalet though, Pilgrim: it never gets easier. You just get quicker. The pros suffer as much as anybody, they just don't take so long about it, OK?

OK. But there's a sense of satisfaction about getting to the top, isn't there?

Oh yes, indeed. There are three specific great things to give you that satisfaction:

1. You don't have to do it again for a few minutes;
2. There is often a lovely view;
3. You usually get to go downhill.

Right: *The top is just round this bend.*

Downhill? I like that bit.

You know what, Pilgrim? Hard to believe, but some people hate it. I think they're just doing it wrong.

What do I need to know about going downhill?

First, get low. This is what drop handlebars were designed for: going downhill fast. Get your hands right in the hooks, like you're milking a cow, so you can reach the brakes and you're not going to slip off the end of the greasy teat, if you will.

Got it. Milking the cow.

Milking the cow. Getting down and flat will make you more aerodynamic, but it will also lower your centre of gravity and increase your stability. Next,

relax. I know that this is difficult at 50mph with only 0.3 of a millimetre of Lycra between your arse and John McAdam's most famous invention, but it will be paradoxically safer if you do. Not only will you soak up the bumps easier with your legs and arms supple, you'll avoid the worst excesses of neckache too. Stay loose, but grip the bars securely. Rather than sitting flat on the saddle, push your weight to the back of it and grip the nose between your thighs.

Should I have the brakes on all the time?

The safest way to go round a corner is with the brakes off, so you're not affecting the grip of the tyres on the road when you're trying to lean the bike over. The logical assumption is thus that you need to get your braking done before you get to the corner. Enter the bend at the speed that you want to go round it. It's very difficult to steer and brake hard simultaneously. Just ask Ayrton Senna.

Control your speed for the corners?

Yes. And the Guide advises against the old adage of braking mainly with the rear. In my experience this just makes you more likely to skid. Fun when you're an eleven-year old trying to impress the girls before assembly, deadly when you're a 40-year-old with a Colnago and a mortgage. Use both brakes together, gently. Remember: if it's wet, they will take a second to clear water from the rim before they bite. When it's like that, don't brake harder, brake earlier.

It'll be fun, right?

It will. If you really want to know how to descend, get on YouTube and find a clip of the 1992 Milan–San Remo. Sean Kelly, past his imperious best at 36, is well short of Moreno Argentin's rear wheel as they top the short climb of the Poggio with just the descent separating him from victory. Argentin's look of shock at seeing the Irishman appearing out of nowhere to outsprint him is one of cycling's great moments. Or maybe it was just the shock of seeing an all-time great wearing the worst helmet ever.

Left: *Milking the cow. Descending in Provence.*

Right: *Rampy hills, like White Down in Surrey, call for bursts interspersed with rests.*

Overleaf: *Tackling the upper hairpins of the breathtaking Bealach na Bà, or Cow Pass, in remote Wester Ross.*

is for Italiano

Colnago. Pinarello. De Rosa. Bianchi, at a push. There are some bikes that are good, there are some bikes that are crap, there are some that are functionally brilliant, and there are some that are made especially for you, but if you want a cool bike it just has to be Italian. The same goes for the moving parts. Shimano works effortlessly, SRAM is the understated functional favourite of the professional, Mavic wheels roll under any discerning rider. But if you need it to be cool, it has to be Campagnolo. Sorry, we don't make the rules.

Hush now, Pilgrim. We enter the inner sanctum.

Wow. It's like the crypt of a cathedral in here. I can almost smell the incense.

Yes, that's lithium grease in the air.

What is this place?

This is the place we come to when we need to commune with the greater power. The place where we kneel before the craftsman's altar. The place where we channel our thoughts into praising all that we stand for in life. This, Pilgrim, is Bob's workshop.

Awesome.

Mmm. Breathe it in. Half a century of maturing rubber, softening steel and non-synthetic lubrication.

Is everything in here Italian?

Not everything, no. It is best to view Italian workmanship as the benchmark, the standard. Other people can do it too, but with the Italians, it's effortless. Look at this.

It's beautiful. It looks like a glass of prosecco on wheels. What is it?

That, Pilgrim, is a 1976 Chesini. Forged in the Veneto, the furnace of twentieth-century artisan bike building. In the industrial hinterland around Verona between the wars, frame builders juggled steel tubes and welding goggles until they learned how to craft the world's most beautiful bicycles. Across northern Italy, men like Giovanni Pinarello, Ernesto Colnago and Ugo De Rosa rose from this artisan explosion to shape the world's finest bicycles through the second half of the twentieth and on into the twenty-first century. Those craftsmen and their art and techniques live on today in the welding workshops of small companies run by the likes of Dario Pegoretti and Roberto Billato.

Those guys knew what they were doing, eh?

Yeah, and there's another guy from the Veneto who had a few things to say about bike design too.

Who's that?

He was a bike racer back in the twenties, back when the sport was growing from a curious middle-class pastime through the epic tales of endurance into the working-class sport of the European masses that has entertained millions. Like many of us, he spent long, lonely hours in the saddle

Below: This bike belongs to somebody who cleans it more often than he rides it.

Right: That's Gimondi and Merckx, son. Look and learn.

thinking. In his case, not thinking about girls, or football, or whether he'd shut the garage door, but how to make bike riding better.

What do we owe this guy?

If you've ever changed gear, it's down to him. He invented derailleur gears.

Blimey, that's pretty major.

That's not all. Ever taken a wheel off without using a spanner?

Of course.

He patented the quick release hub in 1930.

Who was he?

His name was Tullio Campagnolo.

Bit of a dude?

I'll say. When he died in 1983, aged 81, Eddy Merckx delivered the eulogy. Big Ted never rode anything but Campagnolo for all his famous victories. In Britain, you were a dude if you had 'Campag' on your bike; right back to the post-war cycling boom it's been coolest. Americans called it 'Campy'. There's a story that Tullio himself was outraged about these shortenings of his family name, until somebody pointed out that the contemporary British prime minister, Harold MacMillan, was widely known as Supermac. He took it as a compliment from that point on.

So why do so many people use Shimano components then?

Left: *A Giant, Trek and Specialized-free zone*

It's pretty simple, Pilgrim. They work really, really well. In the last 30 years, they've probably been more innovative than Campagnolo, largely thanks to their immense contribution to the development of the mountain bike. So much useful stuff that we use now started life as a mountain bike idea: indexed gears, cassette hubs, combined levers for braking and shifting. The race to be better between the manufacturers has been of massive benefit to us. There are loads of great reasons to ride Shimano componentry. The cassette hub meant we could have more gears. Indexed levers meant we could change them more precisely. Integrated brake and gear levers meant we could change them without taking our hands off the hoods. Electric shifting made it all more effortless.

Campagnolo had to pull their finger out then?

Yes. Back in the day, they'd been the true progenitors of bike tech, now they were playing catch up to the Japanese. It's the story of European manufacturing in a nutshell. Where Campag are clever, though, is

their knack of turning people on. Every time Shimano come up with something new, Campagnolo take it and come up with a cooler version. Their cassette hub purred. Their indexed levers clunked pleasingly. Their derailleurs had little sheets of carbon fibre on them. Their integrated levers didn't have cables poking out of them. Their electronic stuff is just damn fancy. The problem is that most of it doesn't work as well. They don't bother with making sure that their old customers can still use their old kit with the new gear by building in a bit of backwards compatibility. And it's well expensive too.

So why use Campagnolo then?

It's Italian. Have you not been listening?

Left: *A quick-release skewer and a derailleur bearing their inventor's name.*

Below: *Like a 1950s sweet shop for bike nerds.*

J is for Job

When you push back that carefully adjusted swivel chair from your extra-large desk and close down the PC properly, shutting each Excel sheet, saving each set of figures, your mind starts to wander. Why do this every day? Why look at these numbers, despite the food it puts on the table for your family? Why work your fingers to the bone just so you can upgrade your house to the next SW postcode along? Surely, for a man so committed to cycling and his bike (the singular nomenclature is apocryphal; it is assumed you have a number of these objects), the only correct path would be to turn your back on a career such as yours and plough all your money into a boutique bike shop. Only selling cool things. No Raleighs, no hybrids, no kids' bikes, no baskets. No yellow Altura commuter jackets. Just cool stuff. Brilliant.

What do you do for a living, Pilgrim?

Pretty dull, really. I'm a business analyst for a firm of . . .

Stop! Stop already. Some sort of businessy stuff. Fine. Do you like it?

It's OK, I suppose.

What would you like to do?

Well, it's a bit of a pipe dream, I guess, but since I took up the cycling, I've been thinking about giving it all up and opening a bike shop.

Oh yeah? What kind of bike shop?

A nice one. You know, one that sells all the lovely little bits and pieces and cool bikes that we like.

Hmm. Listen carefully.

OK.

Hear that?

Hear what?

You can't hear anything?

No.

That's because what you can hear, Pilgrim, is the sound of my silent fury.

Ah. I take it that you don't think opening a boutique bike shop is a good idea, then?

Let me ask you something about these bits and pieces you want to sell. You're aiming at the sort of things you like to buy, yeah?

Yes, cool stuff.

By cool stuff, you mean nice designs, crafted and unusual limited edition things, a bit obscure and exclusive?

Yes, that's it, the sort of stuff it's hard to get hold of.

By hard to get hold of, do you mean that you don't see it in shops very often?

Err . . . yes, I suppose I do.

Why do you think that is, Pilgrim?

Umm . . . I don't know.

It's because nobody buys it, Pilgrim. Sometimes, a bike shop lucky enough to have a few guys like you for customers might get persuaded into bringing in the odd piece.

A hand-welded titanium bottle cage in the shape of a dragonfly. A front light from Northwest Oregon that is bright enough to burn holes in car windscreens. A tweed jacket made out of the eyebrows of Scottish crofters dispossessed during the Clearances. A bike made out of melted-down Fabergé eggs. Any old emperor's-new-bike bits as long as they cost more than a house in the Cotswolds.

Left: *Sneak a day off work mid-week if you want the road to yourself.*

But, Guide, people like me, we like that kind of thing.

Yes, you like it; accepted. Agreed. What you really like to do is go into that bike shop, see some of this stuff – let's say, a saddle made out of dodo's eggshells – pick it up, coo over it for a while, tell the guy in the shop how delighted you are he's got it in, talk about yourself and how much bike riding you've been doing lately while he's been sweating away in his cripplingly expensive little retail unit, then piss off home without buying it.

I buy that stuff sometimes.

I'll give you that, Pilgrim; you do buy it sometimes. Sometimes, once you've got home after waltzing out of that guy's shop, leaving him mystified as to why you failed to make a purchase after lavishing such adoring

praise on his new delivery of brake callipers cunningly fashioned from an alloy of rocking-horse shit and hen's teeth, you'll order yourself a pair online.

Well, if his price isn't competitive, what does he expect?

Good point, Pilgrim. Because the price of having a high-street retail shop in the same SWdickhead postcode as your friends' Edwardian townhouses and staffing it with professionals knowledgeable enough to nod at the right places when you witter on about the suitability of using your maturing Clement No. 1s for the New Forest sportive you're considering this weekend is very similar to the cost of running a shed full of boxes and a daily Parcelforce collection staffed by trained monkeys in North Garthensthwaiteshire. Which is where that web page is run from.

Are you OK? Guide? Take a deep breath. You've gone a funny colour.

OK. OK. Let me change tack. Let me ask you a different question: what are your qualifications for running a bike shop?

Well, I've got a few quid in the bank.

What's the best way to ensure that your new bike shop has a million pounds in its account at the end of your first year of trading?

I'm listening.

Start with two million in there.

Ah.

What else qualifies you?

I'm passionate about bikes.

True, that is very helpful if you're spending a lot of your time selling things to bicycles.

Huh?

Being 'into' bikes – I have refused to use the widely abused 'passionate' since hearing that a job candidate was 'passionate about waste collection' – is a great qualification for being a mechanic. However, to get the bike's owner to spend some money – most bikes not being known for their earning potential – your understanding needs to be focused on the rider.

Left: *Don't touch what you can't afford, son. Look with your eyes, not your hands.*

Right: *If you want to stop starting and start stopping, these will do the trick.*

You need to like people, not bikes. Tell me, Pilgrim, how do you get on with the people at work?

If I'm honest, they're probably one of the reasons I dream of getting out and opening a shop.

And you enjoy spending long hours with family and friends?

The fact that I spend so much time on my bike would appear to run counter to that statement.

In that case, how are your mechanical skills?

I once fixed a puncture and managed to get home before dark.

I see. Let's go back to your local bike shop man and his uncompetitive pricing for a second.

I just want him to help me out a bit, recognise that I'm a good customer and give me a good price. You know, a special deal.

How much did you spend in Waitrose last month, Pilgrim?

Wow, I wouldn't like to think.

And is it the cheapest supermarket?

No.

Did you by any chance ask for a discount when you reached the checkout?

Well, no.

Despite the fact that you see yourself as a good customer? Let me ask you this, then: how many pounds per hour do you think you spend in Waitrose compared to your local bike shop?

I see what you're saying. You may have a point, Guide. But I just want him to help me.

Let us imagine that, heaven forbid, this fellow keeps dropping his drawers and selling his items for ever shrinking margins until his business is unsustainable and he closes his doors for the last time. Who is going to straighten your rear mech hanger for nothing after you've put it into your spokes for the umpteenth time? Halfords? Toys R Us?

I don't think I want a bike shop any more.

If you want to make money, Pilgrim, get a furniture shop. If a bike shop did a half-price-sale-with-nothing-to-pay-until-2053 type deal, they'd be out of business in a week. That's where the real profitable margins are. Or, better still, get back to those spreadsheets. Your country needs business analysts.

OK, Guide, I get it.

All part of the service, Pilgrim.

Just one thing though: that stuff about having to like people to run a bike shop.

Yes?

Is that why you haven't got one?

Left: *Richmond Park, the most popular destination for London cyclists of all persuasions.*

Overleaf: *The wide open skies over Exmoor's Stoke Pero Common, accessed via some of England's hardest climbs.*

K is for Kit

Welcome to the poseurs' club. Now, let's see . . . Sky team kit? If you don't work for Sky, you've failed the entry policy. Sorry. Nineties professional team kit? You're French. Garish but geometric modern kit bearing the name of a garage or bakery? You're Belgian. Ridiculous technicolour psychedelia explosion featuring the improbable jokey name of a Colorado bike fettler? You're American. Rapha? Stop reading those trendy magazines and get out on your bike some time, and try going further than Richmond Park. Assos? Please, let me get the door for you, come on in.

Right then, Pilgrim. Let's have a look at you. Stand up straight, lad.

What are we looking at?

What you've got on. Yes . . . not bad, not bad at all.

What should I be avoiding?

I hardly know where to start. I guess the first thing is to weigh up the suitability of each item to the task you're asking it to perform and to the current climatic conditions.

The shorts in the snow brigade?

That's a good way of putting it. But have a little empathy for that guy. Let's remember that for some people, their cycling kit is their cycling kit. They have a pair of shorts, a jersey and a rain jacket, and that's what they wear when they go cycling. It's not necessarily the case that they're poorer than you; they have merely elected to spend their earnings on less important things. Like food for their children, or a roof over their heads. You, Pilgrim, are much more likely to suffer from a diametrically opposing problem.

What's that?

Too Much Kit Syndrome. When you are half an hour late getting out on your bike because you couldn't decide which pair of arm warmers to wear, you are suffering from TMKS. That feller wearing shorts for his Hogmanay ride doesn't even know what a pair of arm warmers are, so he's hardly likely to find himself standing in front of the mirror trying and discarding pair after pair.

I, err, I may have done something like that.

You're blushing, Pilgrim. Now, let us confront the conundrum of replica professional team kit. Are you interested in football at all, Pilgrim?

I follow Tottenham. From a distance.

Oh, I'm sorry, what a shame. Never mind. Do you wear a replica shirt ever?

My mum buys me one for Christmas every year, usually with an unsuitable name on the back. I expect I'll get Bale this year.

Left: *You have to get out and ride, if only to justify your outrageous kit expenditure.*

Below: *You can't have too many caps.*

How often do you wear it?

In public? Virtually never. At the one or two games I go to a season, if I'm not going there from somewhere else. And usually under my coat.

Apart from that it's on the sofa for your Spursday evening games on ITV4 against Trabsponzor?

That's pretty much it. Though we'll be in the Champions League next year.

Keep telling yourself that, Pilgrim. My point is that your allegiance to your club isn't one that you feel the need to shout from the rooftops at every opportunity, like a Brit in Marbella. It's a personal thing, a bit like religion or family for most folk. And a football club that you've been brought up with is an earthy, spiritual, visceral companion. A professional cycling team, by way of a contrast, is a wholly commercial enterprise, owned by a sponsor who can come and go. The name on Spurs shirts is but an advertising hoarding. The name on cycling kits is the name of the team. Pledging your love for a commercial company that you don't work for while riding your bike is incongruous at best.

But I like Sky.

That's not unreasonable, Pilgrim. The US Postal Service showed us that it's possible to tap into nationalistic support, especially in countries where a global presence is a new experience, as Sky and GreenEDGE have realised. So, if you feel the need, go for it. But – and this is a big but – it had better be matching. A Sky jersey with Cannondale shorts is a shocking *faux pas*. It demonstrates that you have no allegiance for a team, merely awful taste in bike wear.

I think I'll stay away from replica kit.

Good lad. Now, do you ever feel embarrassed about wearing cycling kit?

Well, I suppose that there have been times when I've walked into a pub or café in my gear, and I'd rather have been wearing a pair of jeans.

The Guide understands. You have inadvertently hit upon a golden truth. Cycling kit looks inherently stupid when not accompanied by a bicycle. There are two lessons you can take from this incontrovertible fact, Pilgrim. The first is that you should obviously keep your bike near to you at all times. The second is that stuff designed for cycling is fine for cycling. We've all seen the guy who feels the need to wear a pair of football shorts over his cycling shorts. He has come to the conclusion that cycling shorts look stupid because he is unconsciously picturing himself wandering around town on a Saturday night in skimpy Lycra. In fact, it is him that looks foolish and is unwittingly drawing the very kind of opprobrium he seeks to avoid by wearing something patently unsuited to the job in hand.

What about colours, Guide?

Left: *You promise I'm not going to see this in TK Maxx next week?*

Right: *Make sure your toes have got some wriggle room when you're buying new shoes.*

That's a harder one to answer, Pilgrim. There is obviously a case for ensuring that you're adequately visible to other road users. The Guide would like to point you towards good lighting to ram this point home. However, on the subject of lurid clothing, we must remember that the models and professionals who look good in this kind of thing are svelte impalas without a hair on their bodies. It's not enough to be fit to look like a pro – you have to be thin. And many of us, I'll venture to say the vast majority of us, are not thin. For the great swathe of middle-aged men, white shorts are a definite and absolute no. Instant, massive fail.

What's next?

Shorts. You can't spend too much money on a pair of shorts, as the quality of your shorts has an instant and immeasurable impact on your ride experience. These must be bib shorts, the type that come up over your shoulders. I know they're scarily reminiscent of Saturday afternoons in the seventies watching Mick McManus going for three falls or submissions on *World of Sport*, but there's no need to worry. This is what all proper cyclists wear; you just can't tell because they've got a jersey over the top half. There are lots of good reasons for bibs, the primary one being that everything stays in place. Get out of the saddle for a quick sprint uphill in more traditional bum wear and you may find yourself sitting back down to a snack of crushed nuts.

Ow.

Damn right, ow. They also give you a better fit, keep your kidneys warm on a rainy day, and avoid the need for an uncomfortably tight drawstring around your waist. A word of warning though, Pilgrim: don't ever, *ever*, wear your bib shorts over the top of your jersey. That is an instant fail.

Roger.

You're welcome, Pilgrim. Now, let us turn our attention to your feet. This is an area where cycling has something in common with golf.

Really? How's that then?

It is possible to enjoy a round of golf with rubbish clubs, but not with uncomfortable shoes. Cycling is much the same; it doesn't matter how nice your bike is, bad shoes will ruin your ride.

So what are the best shoes?

Manufacturers of shoes will give you all sorts of reasons why their shoe is better than another, but it comes down to fit. The shoes that fit you best *are* the best. On the subject of fit, when you're trying them on, don't get them too tight. Your feet will swell up over the course of a ride, so they'll need room, or cramp is a certainty.

I've heard that mountain bike shoes are better?

The benefit of mountain bike shoes is that you can walk in them. Did you buy this bike to go walking?

No.

No, Pilgrim, you bought it to go bike riding. At a push, a case can be made for using mountain bike pedals and shoes for specific things, such as the cobbled bergs of Flanders where you may be forced to walk, but if you're setting out to ride, then road shoes are what you want. They're stiffer with a broader platform on the pedal, so you get more power and a little more comfort on a longer ride. And while you're at it, splash out on some cycling socks. There's nothing worse than the utilitarian sports sock with a cycling shoe. OK, ready?

For anything.

Right: You'll want a good pair of shorts between your rear end and the pavé of Paris–Roubaix.

L is for Legs

When every season begins, we think to ourselves: I'm old; I'm fat; I was never any good even when I was young and slim; I definitely won't be shaving my legs this year. We pootle around the lanes in the watery wintry sunshine in our Roubaix tights happily enough, then spring arrives, and, eventually, that first day where it's warm enough to wear shorts. We take a bracing lungful of Easter air and roll off from the garden gate, grinning in the April sun, until our gaze goes down to those bare knees . . . Oh God. The smooth black Lycra ends in a disgraceful fuzz of man hair. We choke back the nausea rising in our throats, commit a hasty shameful U-turn and run up the stairs three at a time until our shaking hand settles upon a Gillette Fusion. When we're finished, we might even sneak a drop of our partner's St Tropez onto our nightmarishly white calves.

We haven't spoken about the big question yet, have we, Pilgrim?

No.

What are your feelings?

I suppose I go through stages of wondering what it's all about. I don't know what you'd call it, spirituality maybe; whether there's a purpose to everything; whether there's a higher power ... I don't really subscribe to any orthodox traditional religion. You could say it's about fate, but then I don't really want to believe in fate, I want to believe that our actions have an impact on the future, not that

we're just pawns. Maybe karma would be a better way of putting it; what goes around comes around, that sort of thing. Do good things and good things will happen to you.

That's nice. Not the big question I had in mind though.

Oh right. Why didn't you stop me?

Well, your cod primary-school philosophy was pretty funny. What do you think happened to the dinosaurs by the way?

Piss off. What's this big question?

Are you going to shave your legs or not?

I won't pretend that I haven't thought about it.

Let's run over the reasons why racing cyclists do it, and have been doing it for as long as people have been racing bikes. Let's debunk a key myth straight away: it's not for aerodynamics. Let the civilians think that if they want. We know different. There are three main advantages to having shaved legs.

What's the first one?

If you crash when you have hairy legs, the road rash you get is likely to turn your shins into a matted bloody mess, create a high risk of infection and take an age to heal up. If those calves are smooth when you scrape them down the tarmac, any injuries will be a fair bit neater and will heal up a lot quicker.

Roger that.

The second advantage to having shaven legs is one that benefits you and one other person who is intimate with your flesh. No, Pilgrim, not *that* person. I think we've already established that kissy-kissy time is not eating into your schedule at present and we'll come to what women think of your hairless body in a minute. I'm talking about your masseur. Few sports rely on massage as heavily as professional cycling, largely because of its unique blend of ridiculous endurance and lack of impact. If you're doing it right, impact isn't something that should be part of your daily routine. The intense long-term effort married to the lack of smacking into the ground or other people means that a massage to rub away the miles means more and goes further than it would in many contact sports, where massage is more akin to physiotherapy than relaxation. Your masseur will thank you for having smooth legs. His or her hands will penetrate

Right: *Sunshine feels even better on smooth legs.*

the muscles much more readily and bring the relief you seek.

So shaving benefits both the rider and the masseur?

Yes. One thing though: don't ever go for a massage with stubbly legs. It's like sandpaper for the poor bugger that no amount of whale song or panpipes will soothe. Oh, and please, please, please . . . do *not* ask for a happy ending.

Move on, please.

The third reason for shaving your legs is less tangible and more rarely spoken about, but it's no less real for all that. In fact, if we're being honest, it's by far the most popular and significant factor that lead those cyclists who shave to do it. You do it to show you're serious, that you mean business. It shows your

dedication: not just that you can take the time to do it, not just that you're prepared to suffer all sorts of social exclusion. It is a visual demonstration of the effort you put into your riding. We can all see those rippling, chiselled muscles now. Bang. You're a star.

So do I shave? Wax? Err . . . electrolysis? How do you do it?

The first time you shave is a complete pain, Pilgrim. I won't lie to you. Pushing a disposable Bic through the untamed primeval forest of your legs is a task that Sisyphus wouldn't fight you for. It's lucky they come in packs of ten. Much better if you can reduce the workload before the real shaving gets started. A crop down to stubble with hair clippers will make the final cut much easier. If you don't have clippers, then hair removal cream will clear the way, but it tends to leave some wispy patches, so you'll have to shave afterwards anyway. Plus, it stinks to high heaven and leaves your legs feeling like you've been paddling at Chernobyl.

Can you cut yourself?

Yes, you can, but using a better quality razor and some shaving foam will protect you to a certain extent and give you a better shave too. Ask Roger Federer. The iffy bits are the backs of your ankles and knees. The trick is to take the weight off that foot so your tendons aren't strained and shave upwards. If you like to have a bath once or week or so, that's the time to get out the blade. It won't take long; just put your copy of Miranda Hart's *Is It Just Me?* down for five minutes, your skin will be soft from a soak in hot water, and you can float a leg to avoid the ankle getting ridgey and attracting a snick.

So it's not too much hassle?

After that first Amazonian deforestation session it's a piece of cake. A quick sprint up the calves and thighs whenever you have a shower, or a once-weekly concerted scalping. Put some moisturiser on as soon as you get out of the water; baby oil before the towel is a good rule. It's a great excuse for having all sorts of feminine oils and creams in the bathroom. And should anybody ask if the reason you shave your legs is because, at the weekends, you're called Davina, just tell them you're a cyclist. There's many a closeted transgendered beauty with a racing bike gathering dust in the shed. It's a great beard.

Really?

No idea, Pilgrim. I was winging that last bit.

Umm ... how far up do you go?

Left: *The road skirting the Assynt coastline is one of Scotland's hidden gems.*

Right: *What's the betting that their razors are vintage, too?*

A common question. Most folks' hair thins out on their upper thighs, so that's a good place to stop. If you're a little more simian, you'll just have to make your own mind up. Fashion yourself a pair of hair knickers with a frilly bottom if you like. I would say though, that just taking the hair down to the short line robs you of one of the pleasures of having smooth legs: they are much more comfortable under Lycra than the original version of you. The snug fabric doesn't tug on shaved skin like it does on wiry flesh.

Do girls like it?

That's subjective. If you find one who rides a bike, you're much more likely to find an understanding eye. Otherwise, if your lovely partner can be persuaded to actually allow the act to occur, you'll probably find that she actually doesn't mind it as much as she thought she would. She might even prefer the silky touch when push comes to shove. Don't climb into bed with stubble though: girls absolutely hate that. All girls. The most difficult moment is breaking the news that you're considering shaving in the first place. I advise just doing it, as a kind invitation of her opinion tends to elicit a reaction that ranges from a patronising smirk through degrading cackles to a horrified shriek. Bag packing is not unknown, although this tends to be a straw-and-camel's-back situation. Put it this way: if you've spent the weekend on a stag weekend in Prague and come back two days late with a tattoo, an eye-watering credit card bill and an STD, don't choose that week to shave your legs.

Below: *Wear that plumbing with pride.*

Right: *If I put my head down, I can just make Boots before closing time.*

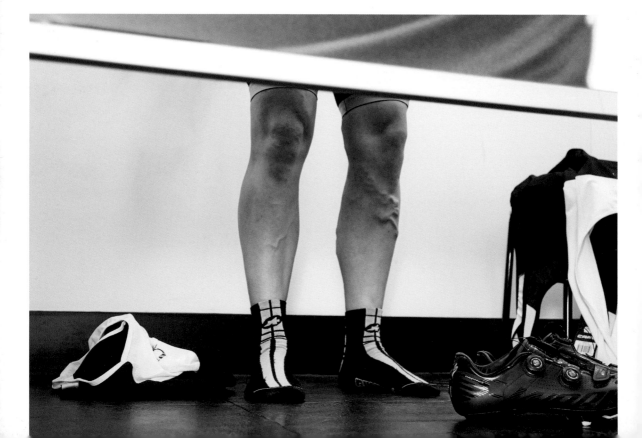

M is for Mileage

One very important delineation between the pro and the amateur is that the former will always give you his ride details in time rather than yardage. Thus, when asked 'How far did you ride yesterday?', never be tempted into working out the actual distance covered. No, no, no. The answer should always be along the lines of 'Three hours'. Even better is a nonchalant shrug and a frowning 'Just six hours, steady. Had to be back to pick Josh up from rugby practice.' You may resort to actual physical distances when the time elapsed runs beyond weeks, that is, 'I only managed five thousand kilometres last month. Bloody work, eh?' Note the use of kilometres over clunky old imperial miles.

Some people will tell you that there is no substitute for 'getting in the miles', Pilgrim. They're not wrong. But I suggest that we take the concept to the next level.

The next level, Guide?

The next level. Far from being a means to an end, 'getting in the miles' *is* the end. That's what we're here for. Life is not a rehearsal. You're not getting in the miles to prepare for something else, you're getting in the miles because that's what you do. That's what you're here for. To get in the miles.

I like that message.

Good. We can – in fact we should – call it training, because that's what we call any bike riding that's not done as part of an event of some kind, but let's not kid ourselves. The real reason we want to ride for six hours in the Cotswolds on Sunday is because we want to spend all day on our bikes somewhere lovely. Yes, OK, it will better prepare us for sporting targets yet to come, but the real point of the expedition is not some sort of deferred satisfaction down the road. No. This is real, raw instant gratification.

So the term 'training' is a little bit on the euphemistic side?

That's up to you, Pilgrim. If it helps motivate you to get out there when your bed feels warm and snuggly or the darts are on the telly, then allow yourself to imagine how horrible that sportive with 15,000 feet of climbing will be if you don't get some preparation in right now. But never forget the bottom line. Repeat after me: it's meant to be fun.

It's meant to be fun.

Let the mantra stand.

When do I decide that it's not fun? What if it's raining?

We're all different, Pilgrim. For some of us, riding in the rain is a spiritual, life-affirming experience, especially when we consider how many others have taken the downpour as a quite literal sign from above that today is a good day to stay indoors and work their way through that *Breaking Bad* box set that's been gathering dust. Then there are those among us who regard a wet bike ride as about as desirable as being an *X Factor* contestant consigned to Louis Walsh's team. Or drinking piss out of a broken glass. The feeling is much the same. It's pretty much universally accepted that going out into the rain is a lot worse than if it begins to rain while you're already out there. With that in mind, you're allowed a pass if it is actually raining when you're due to leave. You can still go if you want, but don't beat yourself up if you decline. Remember the mantra . . .

It's meant to be fun.

Bingo. A good helper in preparing yourself mentally for a morning ride is to make sure that everything is ready the night before. Pump your tyres up, drop a thread of lube on your chain. Lay your kit out on a chair next to the bed. The fewer choices and chores

Left: *Longer hills demand a controlled effort.*

Right: *The view is always better when you've ridden up.*

you have before the off, the easier it will be to roll out. And you'll sleep better too.

I suppose having the right gear helps.

Damn straight. I have had the urge to cause instant and lasting bodily harm to many a bike shop worker who has suggested that there is no such thing as unsuitable weather, merely unsuitable clothing, but there is a grain of truth in that. If you've spent £200 on a nice rain jacket, the rain is a validation of that expense, and a chance to wear a treasured item. And those white oversocks you bought online that perform no discernible task other than make you look *well* Belge can have a run out too.

What do you think about on those long solo mileage days?

Cycling as an activity takes up just the right amount of front-brain power to clear your mind. All the irritating juggling and competing worries, nags, plans, dreams and things you're trying to remember don't have the space to come out and play like they do when you're trying to sleep, trying to drive or pretending to work. There's really only room for one constant train of thought, so you can just let it run. It's rare to get bored if you're out in the countryside. There will be times in the city where a bit more concentration is needed and flights of fancy are necessarily put on hold. Conversely, if you've got a turbo trainer or a set of rollers, you might have room for some of those unwelcome thoughts to crowd back in. In those cases you may find it useful to mentally put all The Smiths' albums in chronological order. *Hatful Of Hollow* counts as a real new record, by the way, while *Louder Than Bombs* and *The World Won't Listen* don't.

Above: *Company is rarely unwelcome, even when it wears white shorts.*

Right: *If you've gone out to do four hours, don't come home after three.*

Motivation for indoor training is harder.

It all comes back to mileage. Set yourself a mental target for the week and plan your time. If it looks like you're going to fail to meet it on the road, it's time to spin the wheels without going anywhere. Rollers will hold your concentration anyway, as you're likely to fall off and fuck up your living room if not yourself if you drift off. If you're going down the route of the turbo trainer, set it up in front of the telly and get a subscription to Sky Sports. There's always something on, and you don't need to hear it. If it's football, try lifting the intensity until the ref blows the whistle or the ball goes out of play, then resting until it happens again. The hours will fly by. Don't try this with rugby though. The ref's whistle never shuts up. He has to wear a bloody microphone just for us to have a clue what's going on his head. You won't know if you're coming or going.

My turbo is in the garage.

Ah, motivation and filling the mind is more problematic. Again, I turn to the arts. I advise putting the films of Tarantino into order based on quality, then trying to recite the plot of each through memory. Trying to decide whether *Django* beats *Jackie Brown* is a tough call.

I thought Pulp Fiction *and* Reservoir Dogs *were the best ones.*

Well, obviously. But that's not going to fill an hour, is it?

Left: *Have you ever gone out and wished you hadn't? Didn't think so.*

Overleaf: *Italian road builders take the prize for using the contours of the land to keep gradients steady.*

N is for No

There are some things that the cyclist must have no truck with.

Simply unacceptable.

Just say 'No!'

I don't want to sound negative, Pilgrim, but no.

No?

No. There are times when we must take a stand against iniquities, misdemeanours, style crimes, mistakes and downright foolishness. The Guide is about to give you a list of things you must avoid at all times without question or pause. These aren't opinions, these are immutable and unforgivable felonies. I don't suggest for one moment that you yourself are a proponent of any of these foul practices, Pilgrim. This is merely a word to the wise.

A cautionary tale. A *Diet of Worms* for the twenty-first-century bike rider, if you will.

I ain't eating no hermaphrodite invertebrates, no matter what you say.

No, Pilgrim, I meant the sixteenth-century rules laid down by Martin Luther.

Huh? The civil rights guy? 'I have a dream' and all that?

No, Pilgrim, no. Martin Lu— Look, forget that, just shut up and listen. This stuff is crucial. Got it?

Got it, sorry.

Some of these we've talked about already, but they're worth reiterating in an effort to have a checklist to refer to. A 'No!' list. So, in no particular order, 'No!' number one is non-matching tyres. If I catch you with a Michelin on the front and a Conti on the back, you'd better have a damn good reason. And if they're different colours . . . Ooh, that's just sent a cold shiver down my spine. While we're on the subject of matching, let's extend this one. Pretty much anything on your bike that you have two of should be matching. Wheels. Brake cables. Gear cables. Bottles. OK?

Non-matching bits. Check.

'No!' number two: nodding. Sit still for God's sake. In a practical sense, every action has an opposite

reaction, so you're losing power bobbing about anyway. But more importantly you look like a total dick. Nodding is a big enough crime that bike shop folk will call ill-informed customers 'nodders', and that is plenty reason enough alone to avoid it. Feel free to use the term as a mild derogatory insult to any fool that interrupts your day with inept behaviour. Standing still on the left-hand side of an escalator? Nodder. Lorry drivers that pull out to overtake other lorries on the M6 then sit neatly alongside each other for ten miles at a steady 56mph? Nodders. People who say 'Now, I don't like much comedy, but I'll tell you who's funny, that Lee Evans.' Nodders. People

Above: *Oi, Rooney, you've forgotten your shin pads.*

Right: *Combe Bottom, one of the South's best known climbs. Nodder-free zone.*

who queue for hours to get to the bar, then wonder vacantly what they fancy when they finally get served. Nodders.

Nodding. Check.

Wearing a time-trial helmet unless you're actually, at that precise moment, racing in a time trial. I know, I know, but I've seen it. File with the other helmet crimes: peaks, fitted on the back of your head, loose straps, glasses under the straps . . . Need I go on?

Helmet crimes. Check.

Bad coffee. Life is just too damn short to drink shit coffee. Agent Cooper may never have figured out who killed Laura Palmer, but he was right about the importance of a decent roasted bean. If you stop at a café and they serve you pale dishwater, never go back. Never. And if a friend offers you a coffee at his house and reaches for the instant jar, help a brother out: tell him what a mistake he's making. He'll thank you in the long run, rude as it may seem at the time.

Bad coffee. Check.

No unnecessary accelerations. You've been cruising along in the group as a succession of your friends tap out a steady 18mph on the front that everybody's happy with. When it's finally your turn, don't crank it up to 22mph. You're not proving how strong you are to everybody. You're proving to everybody that you're a wanker. The same thing goes for hills. The bloke who thinks it's OK to sit chatting in the group all morning then overtakes everyone to sprint up the first hill will find himself riding alone with a lot more regularity than covering those vainglorious hundred yards. Curiously, the group will

Right: *How many days do you think this sportive is likely to take you? How many family members are you bringing along?*

meet half an hour earlier at a different café without him getting the message.

Accelerations. Check.

Half wheeling. A not unrelated topic to the last 'No!' but subtly different. The half wheeler doesn't pop out after a nice half an hour in your slipstream and sprint off to make you feel inadequate. He rides next to you, but in front of you at all times. You speed up to catch him; he raises his speed by the same amount, your front tyre always level with his front hub. You slow down to test him; sure enough, he's still half a wheel ahead. In this instance, rest your hand gently on his hip and ease him back until you are level with each other and accompany your actions with a concerted hard stare deep into his eyes. As well as being irritating, half wheeling is dangerous. If you're alongside each other and touch shoulders or flanks, that's all it will be. The half wheeler is great at hooking his bars round your arm to avoid a pothole.

Half wheeling. Check.

Letting your arm warmers slip down so there is an inch of bare flesh showing between the sleeves of your jersey and your wrinkly Lycra: No! In fact, any baggy Lycra. Any baggy kit at all. No! And as for the bloke I saw in the New Forest last week riding in a sleeveless vest – a *sleeveless vest* – and arm warmers? I'm coming for you, mate.

Baggy arm warmers. Baggy anything. Check.

Now, there is something to be said for the benefits of compression clothing in helping your body recover from a tough workout. Some find wearing tight-fitting leggings after an event or a massive ride will make them feel a little less sore the following day. That's fine in the comfort of your own home. But the man who rides his bike in a pair of compression socks . . . Words fail me, Pilgrim. If I have to explain, you will never understand.

Compression socks in public. Check.

Riding through red lights. How can we expect motorists to have respect for us as fellow road users when we can't even abide by the simplest rule that's there to help everybody? Yeah, I know, we probably won't kill anybody, but neither would car drivers if they looked both ways and just edged through pedestrians on empty junctions. But they wouldn't do it, would they? It's not about lovely cyclists versus horrible motorists. There are good people and tossers; sometimes they walk about, sometimes they ride bikes, sometimes they drive cars. You can't tell if they're good or bad by their mode of transport, only by their actions.

Jumping the lights. Check.

I'm getting worked up and running out of space here, Pilgrim. Gold zips. Cafés without cake. White leg warmers. Riding at night without lights. Overshoes with socks. Homemade components. Cold bacon. Twerking. Mumford & Sons. Ashley Young. Nigel Farage. Brighton. Fake boobs. Robbie Savage.

Are you all right, Guide? Would you like a lie down?

Have you seen my angina pills?

Left: *The risks inherent in buying cycling shorts online. They looked all right on the website.*

O is for Objectives

It's always good to have something to aim at. Make sure that at any given moment you have some distant objective to hand in case anybody asks you. Ideally, this will be a long way off in terms of both time and miles, and will also be exotic but traditional. 'I don't want to go into the red this morning, I'm tapering for Lombardia', for instance, is a fantastic excuse for being left behind on Sydenham Hill. 'Wanted to tweak my sprint for Oudenaarde' justifies jumping an amber light at a pedestrian crossing when everybody else has thoughtfully drawn to a halt. Excitedly exclaiming that you 'Can't wait for the London to Brighton!" will be seen as an epic fail

It's an awful lot easier to get yourself up and out when you're actually preparing for something, Pilgrim. Give yourself a target. Something to aim at

Well, funny you should say that, Guide. I've been thinking lately that I gave up my drama school aspirations too soon, and was thinking of joining a local am-dram group.

Let's pretend we didn't hear that and begin again, shall we?

Oops, sorry. I didn't really mean it. Am-dram? Me? No way, not me.

Enough, Pilgrim. Let's find something in the middle distance that you really want to do on your bike. Something that you can look forward to, something that will motivate you to be in the best shape possible when it comes around. It's conversations like this and the resulting daydreams that keep you going through the short, dark winter days with dreams of spring sunshine and the wearing of shorts.

Yes, I can see that, especially in that grim bit of winter when Christmas and New Year are done and it still seems like forever until the clocks go forward.

You start thinking of sunshine and blossom, knee warmers instead of tights . . . That should be enough to get you sweating away on the turbo trainer to remove the excess turkey. Which reminds me, Pilgrim, have you booked your work Christmas do yet? Toni & Guy are doing a special offer: Christmas dinner with all the trimmings.

Christmas dinner with all the trimmings. That's a joke, right, Guide? Good one. I might write that down.

Do that. Now, this ride, this target that is going to sustain you through the long, dark nights that await

on the far side of all that saturnalia. First, we ought to decide how long we're going for. If you have a week or so at your disposal, then place-to-place rides have the kind of epic intention that can be very attractive. The most popular is the end-to-end one: Land's End to John o' Groats. It can be a bit trunk road-ish and not particularly picturesque though if you want to push on and get it done. There are nicer and more technically demanding variations. Glasgow to John o' Groats hugging the coastline of the West Highlands takes about the same amount of time, for instance, but takes in some magnificent roads and some outrageously steep pitches along the way. Further afield, the Raid Pyrénéen is a classic. From the Atlantic to the Med along the French side of the border, crossing every major col on its journey.

Ooh, that sounds like a corker.

Left: *One advantage of home training: there's always plenty of water in the tap.*

Below: *Le Tour de Garage. Must remember to put those golf clubs on eBay.*

Yes, it's beautiful. You can virtually guarantee every type of weather whenever you do it, but early summer is the best. As you climb out of the valleys, it feels as though you're passing through different bands of colour as the mountain flowers change according to your altitude. Stunning. The issue with these destination-to-destination, multiple-day rides is carrying your stuff. You can choose to travel light – I know a girl who rode from one end of Ireland to the other in full race kit with a little black dress rolled up around a pair of flip flops in her jersey pocket for the evenings – or get assistance. If you don't have a handily placed pal who fancies the trip behind the wheel, there are great holiday companies who will guide you, book the hotels and carry all your stuff from day to day. Or, if you don't fancy the aggravation, plonk yourselves somewhere nice for a base and just ride every day. Alpine ski chalets in the summer are made for this, but you lose some of the purpose of the place-to-place journey.

What about shorter trips?

Well, one glance at *Cycling Weekly* will show you that there are any number of local sportives on any given Sunday through the year now. Pick one and go; you can even just turn up on the morning sometimes. Or for more of a target, some do a series, so you can spread your targets out and not have to think about it. Sizeable events mean a weekend away for most of us, and there are some memorable rides out there. There are big days out like the Dragon Ride in Wales, where half the sportive population of Britain turn up, or the super-hard Fred Whitton Challenge, a tour of the Lake District's high passes that leaves no stone unturned or back unbroken. Or, while your mates are on so-called 'mini breaks', try a short flight to the continent and take on the Maratona dles Dolomites for a crack at Europe's most scenic roads.

Right: *The respite between Hardknott and Wrynose Passes in the Lakes.*

In fact, any of the Italian gran fondos are a superb experience; you can even go up and over the iconic Stelvio pass on one. The title of the original sportive event is customarily bestowed upon La Marmotte, held annually at Bourg d'Oisans in the French Alps for the past three decades or so. The tried and tested route takes you over some fearsome Tour de France *hors catégorie* mountains, including the monstrous Col du Galibier and its little brother, the Col du Télégraphe. All of which needs to be conquered before you even start upon the most famous 21 hairpins in sport that lead you to the finish line on Alpe d'Huez.

Is that the most famous sportive then?

La Marmotte might be the oldest, but the one everyone wants to do is l'Étape du Tour. Each year, the Tour de France organisers pick one of the toughest stages of that year's race and run a sportive over the course a few days before the race itself arrives. If you ran a *Family Fortunes* style 'We asked a hundred people to name a cyclosportive event', l'Étape would be the top answer. Well, second probably, after 'What?'

Are all major sportives in the mountains?

One of the best sportives is the awesome Ronde van Vlaanderen, the Tour of Flanders. On the first Sunday in April since time immemorial, the people of Belgium have spilled out into the *laans* of the Flemish Ardennes to watch the world's best cyclists lock horns on the short, steep cobbled bergs that give the famous race its unique character. These days, the sportive rider can ride the event himself the day before, get lashed on Trappist beer on the Saturday night, then watch with a sore head and legs as the pros do it the morning after. A cracking weekend, and only an hour or so from Calais. And if you're in the region, check out the busted farm tracks across the border into France that make Paris–Roubaix such a bunfest. My supposition that there are no great flat bike rides still holds strong; there may not be any hills to speak of on the long run to Roubaix, but it's not flat, it's bumpy beyond belief. They don't call those knackered old cobbles the 'Hell of the North' for nothing.

Hard to decide, eh, Guide?

Think about what you enjoy doing, or what inspires you. If you like the camaraderie and the thrill of a big event, pick one of those monuments. But don't forget these are all public roads; you can go and ride them whenever you want. If you like a bit of peace, either solo or with a few mates, do your research and give it a go. Don't be fooled by this stuff about 'closed roads' that some of them push, either. They're not closed. There are thousands of other people out there on bikes at the same time, most of them with even less idea than you, Pilgrim. Piccadilly Circus in rush hour is probably safer than the first ten kilometres of l'Étape.

Gosh. Tough choice. I think I like the sound of a gran fondo.

Good choice, Pilgrim. It will be a memorable trip, and those enticing Italian vistas will keep you dreaming of spring well beyond the last of the turkey sandwiches. In fact, the food in Italy is so good that I may come with you. Just for moral support and coaching expertise, of course.

Thank you, Guide.

Left: *Cipressas, strade bianche, vintage bike, autumn sunshine … It must be Chianti and l'Eroica.*

P is for Peloton

It snakes through the bends, slithers smoothly up hill and down dale, a myriad of striking colours, seemingly a synergetic blend of the organs of one being working in perfect rhythm with another. A huge murmuration of beating wings; a near-silent swish of saltwater as fins turn in unison.

Or, a jumble of bent wheels, ripped Lycra, grazed knees and a hundred 'it-wasn't-me-it-was-that-twat-over-there's. Your actions will decide.

There's nothing better, Pilgrim. No greater feeling in cycling. Whistling along in a bunch twenty strong or more, two centimetres from the wheel in front, shoulder occasionally brushing against the riders on your left and right. The effort needed to turn the pedals to keep speed with your brothers so infinitesimal it is a whisker away from free wheeling, chatting easily about last week's racing, last night's football, next week's night out.

Riding in the peloton? Scary business, Guide.

But a skill well worth learning, Pilgrim. Essential if you ever want to race, even at the most junior level, and dead handy if you ever take on those big sportives we've been talking about. Bunch riding is dangerous, yes, but wonderful when mastered. Which is why you're so lucky you've got me, eh?

Lead on, Macduff.

Before you learn to ride in the bunch, you need to learn to ride in the line. From there, you will just have to stir in a few extra thoughts and skills, but the line is where you learn without hurting yourself. Like touch rugby.

You can still get hurt playing touch rugby though, can't you?

And you can certainly get hurt riding in the line if you're not careful, but there is a greater margin of error, and fewer people are likely to get hurt in the event of a mistake. So that's where we'll start. Make sense, Pilgrim?

Makes sense, Guide.

The golden rule of riding with other people is one that lion tamers the world over are familiar with: no sudden movements. Don't accelerate quickly, don't steer jerkily, but most importantly, get off those brakes. The guy at the front will only brake if he has to, and he'll shout when he does, so there's no need for you to either. If everybody rides smoothly, you don't need to touch them. The most irritating rider in the line is the one that drops off the wheel in front

because he's scared of riding close, then powers back up because he thinks he's getting dropped, then whacks the anchors on to stop smacking into the back of his pals, thus beginning the entire unhappy chain of events again. If you ever catch a group of guys on the road, you will get a distorted view that says every bunch has one of these guys in it, but that's because either by accident or design, he will end up last in the line. It's impossible to ride behind him. Don't be speeding-up-and-slowing-down-guy, Pilgrim.

I can see that would be really off-putting. Have you got any tips for avoiding being that guy?

Above: *The Watendlath road in the central Lakeland fells is a dead end, but who cares. It's beautiful.*

Right: *If one of us stops, we all stop.*

There are a couple of things. First, don't start too close to the wheel in front. Get a feel for the rhythm of the group and you'll naturally close to within a few inches as you warm to the task and each other's habits. Next, don't stare at the tyre in front of you. It's a natural thing to do – looking down to make sure you don't hit it – but you will find you ride much more smoothly if you look up over his shoulder as if you were at the front of the group. You'll have a wider view, be less inclined to make jerky adjustments, and you'll be more aware of hazards before they become problems.

Look up and look where you're going. Sounds like good advice.

The other huge factor in riding smoothly and consistently is cadence. Do you know what cadence refers to in cycling, Pilgrim?

The speed you pedal at.

Very good. The speed your feet go round at in RPM. Optimally, you want your feet to spin around in circles at a high rate rather than stomping one by one on the pedals. This is a hard knack to master in your early days. A high cadence just gets you bouncing around in the saddle, but pick out the smoothest guy in the line and slip in behind him and match his gear selection. You'll soon get the feel of pedalling circles rather than stomping. Spinning this way makes you much less likely to go steaming into the back of somebody, and will also give you longevity, as you will be expending less energy once you've mastered the art. If you've got a cadence counter, you should be around 100 RPM. Riding on your own, you're more likely to be nearer 85, so practise pushing it up. If you haven't got a bike computer with this facility, find a quiet, flat road on your own and have a stopwatch or a watch with a second hand in view. When a new minute ticks over, count each time your right knee goes round. If it's 50 times in a minute you're bang on. If it's less, drop a gear and try to maintain the same speed.

So good cadence will help me fit in to the bunch?

Exactly, Pilgrim. There is another more advanced trick that pros seem to be able to do as a matter of course but takes a great deal of thought for the rest of us: standing up on the pedals.

Really? I would have thought that was straightforward?

Just doing it, yes, that's easy. However, doing it right is a different matter, and it has a huge impact on whether you can stand up in a bunch or not. You see, Pilgrim, as you stand up on the pedals, you naturally create a dead spot where to anybody riding behind you, your bike seems to lurch back towards them alarmingly. If you've ever tried to ride a fixed wheel bike, you'll find the sensation when you first stand on the pedals very strange indeed. If you need to stand up to stretch your legs or attack a hill, you need to push hard and stand just before your foot comes over the top of the pedal revolution. Easier said than done. I advise thinking very hard before you stand up, as those behind you may not appreciate it.

Thanks, Guide. What about all these hand signals I see people doing?

Hmm. Don't get carried away with them, Pilgrim. You can overdo it. Leave it to the experienced guys up front unless it's an obvious hazard; a shout will often go further than a hand gesture. But here are the main ones.

George Hincapie leads the BMC team on a Belgian training run.

A point with a finger down to either side indicates an approaching hole or obstacle in the road. Not at the hole, but down to the ground on whichever side the hole will be. The gesture should be made well in advance, not while swerving round said obstacle.

A palm held down, flattened towards the road and shaken from side to side indicates generally rough surface approaching.

A left hand held behind your bum wafting outwards from the kerb does not indicate that the rider in front of you has just let one go. He's telling you to pull out to overtake another cyclist or a parked car etc.

Clear shouts are more useful, especially in a bunch. 'Hole!' or 'Braking!' go a long way.

And all of these apply to riding in a line or in a bunch?

Yes. The next step after the line is two lines next to each other. You should never really exceed this on public roads; you'll only piss people off, and we've all got to get along. Be ready to go back to single file quickly if the road narrows or drivers are trying to get past and you can make it easier for them. Make it a rule that the person on the outside of each two abreast goes in front of the one on the inside, then you'll avoid those awkward 'After you, Claude' moments and get the job done quickly and efficiently.

But having riders on all sides is obviously a big jump in terms of danger and skills.

It doesn't have to be. Remember all the rules we've just been through and you should be OK. The real difference in having people on all sides is that your steering has to be spot on. You'll often hear pros complaining about a rider who corners 'like a 50-pence piece'. That's the guy who jerks his way round bends instead of sweeping gently through. You can imagine how difficult he makes it for people around him. I once heard a tale of an English pro who went to Belgium to race for the first time and found himself the target of Flemish curses at every corner until a Belgian hand actually reached across and steered his bars for him through a turn. He gratefully and ashamedly kept his head down and did what he was told.

Am I ready for the peloton, Guide?

I think so, Pilgrim. You're keen and you're careful; I like that. Just one thing: don't you dare let a wheel go.

Let a wheel go?

If you're in a long, fast line, every man hanging on by the skin of his teeth to the man in front, you have a grave responsibility to all those behind you. If you allow a gap to open between you and those in front, you'll be letting a lot of people down. If you get dropped, they get dropped too, despite them faithfully keeping up their side of the bargain. When it feels too hard, just remember this: the pain of staying on that wheel is infinitely preferable to the pain you'll suffer trying to get back on it.

Left: Use the rider in front of you to keep out of the wind.

Overleaf: The infamous hairpins of the mighty Stelvio, skirting Switzerland without leaving Italy.

Q is for Quackery

Hey, here's a brilliant idea: sign up to a coach online. Somebody you've never met, who's never seen you ride a bike or checked your bike set-up. Pay him (no woman would have the front to set herself up as an online cycling coach) a nice chunk of money to tell you that this Saturday you should be doing five hours, steady. Under his remote instruction, perform a series of bizarre complex manoeuvres using one leg at a time on your turbo trainer in the garage while your wife watches *Downton*. Eat beetroot every meal and marvel at your purple pee – just like he said you would. Genius brings its own results. Come on, thousands of triathletes can't be wrong, can they?

There are a lot of charlatans out there, Pilgrim. People who'll gladly take your money to tell you what you're doing wrong.

You think?

I'm not sure I like your tone. Listen: people envy you, son, being able to tap into this deep well of wisdom and experience. People should envy us. I envy us.

What? Don't you mean ...

Never mind, Pilgrim, never mind. All I'm saying is there's a lot of junk out there and you need to be careful. Luckily, you've got the Guide to look after you. But, to paraphrase Dave Prowse in his second most celebrated role, Green Cross Code Man, I won't always be there when you cross the road.

It's hard, Guide. It seems like there's another cycling magazine on the rack at W H Smith every week. If I go online, the world and his wife are telling me what I should or shouldn't be doing. How do I tell the good stuff from the bad?

Information is good, but there is information overload and conflicting information too. The Guide says: read everything, listen to everyone, and then weigh it up. The smart money follows the philosophy that says 'Let's not do it like this just because that's how it's been done for decades, let's do it like this because it works.' Look at the professionals for a pointer. If it's a good idea, they'll probably be doing it; it's their livelihood after all. When I see Mark Cavendish winning sprints in a pair of compression socks, I'll think about wearing them on my bike. Until then, I'll avoid looking like a cock if at all possible.

Do I need a coach?

You're not Andy Murray, Pilgrim. You're not Bradley Wiggins. You don't need a coach. However, a good coach could help you improve and reach your goals whatever they may be, so you could conceivably get something out of working with someone who will set you a programme, look at your technique and measure your progress. But do you *need* him? No, of course not. That knowledge doesn't stop any number of keen MAMILs with money to burn signing up to become disciples of coaches more used to trying to help professional athletes win international titles than commodities traders get round the Gran Fondo Nove Colli. They'll turn up on the Adriatic coast with their spreadsheets and SRM cranks, keen to fill in all their details for later dissection by their coach. They will even have instructions on what sort of power output to maintain during their day out. Keen, eh?

Mmm, let's just say . . . you know, just for the sake of argument and something to talk about, that I would like a coach. What should I be looking for?

The first thing to do to eliminate an unsuitable coach is to find out if he or she wants to see you, Pilgrim. If your discussions with a potential coach don't seem to mention any initial meeting or consultation, it's probably best to walk away. Despite my earlier scaremongering, there aren't actually many dodgy cycling coaches around. The sport of triathlon used to be riddled with people

who would set themselves up as gurus. They were usually running or swimming coaches, and, hey, any fool can ride a bike, right? Preying on the triathlete's tendency to be overwhelmed by taking on three entirely different disciplines, these 'coaches' would offer to set entire programmes for you. So, a guy who spent many years crouching beside a pool, or peeping into the showers, the scent of chlorine forever oozing from his pores, would somehow be qualified to tell you how to ride a bike. And, hey presto, you wouldn't even have to see him; he could do it all by email and bank transfer, you lucky, lucky people.

So what will a good coach do, then?

First, he or she will want to have a good talk to you, or more accurately, get you to talk to him or her. He – let's just accept for the moment it's a man, I know you get sweaty palms and tongue-tied around girls, and this he or she thing is wearing me down – will want to know exactly what you want to achieve through working with him. You can only reach your goals if you know what your goals are.

That makes sense. Then I suppose he gets into all the tests to find out how you're doing. How do they work?

He'll normally have a 'lab' or a 'clinic'. This might be a room in a gym, or perhaps a little industrial unit, hopefully somewhere in the middle of nowhere that you can have a nice ride out to once in a while. It'll be full of computers, but it'll also have static bikes and wires to stick to you, and masks with tubes coming out to cover your face. All for show, obviously. And stuff to calculate your VO2 max or some old shit like that. Sometimes you'll climb on to one of these bikes for your testing, and sometimes your own bike will be fitted to a turbo trainer that is in turn linked up to a bank of computers left over from a *Blake's 7* set.

Right: High above Derwent Water on the way to Ashness Bridge.

Is this what they call a ramp test? What's that all about?

Despite the name, a ramp test doesn't actually take place on a ramp. It's called that because you, as the subject, make a concerted effort over a certain amount of time, usually about twenty minutes. You are then subjected to increasing difficulty during that period. This is usually created by raising the resistance of the turbo that your bike is attached to in stages, thus 'ramping' the intensity. There are different sorts of tests, like lactate threshold tests and FTP (don't ask) tests, but the most talked about one is the MAP test. That stands

for Maximum Aerobic Power. Some people say 'maximal' but that's not a real word in the Oxtail English Dictionary. Using a cadence meter, you ride on a static bike at, say, 90 RPM. To start with, the resistance will be set so that you need to put out, for instance, 150 watts of power to rev at 90 RPM. With me so far?

I'm following. I presume they increase that intensity, giving you the 'ramp'?

Yes. Every three minutes, the computer will increase the resistance by another 30 watts, so you have to up your effort to keep your revs at 90. After about twenty minutes, the sweat will be pissing out of you and you'll be seriously questioning your sanity, having realised that you've actually paid somebody good money to torture you. The figure that this will eventually generate, a figure that will often be spouted endlessly by the self-absorbed subject, is the amount of power they were putting out just before they collapsed. Yes, that's effectively what a MAP test is. You go as hard as you can until you die, and record the amount of energy you were expending just before your eyes closed and your toes curled up. You remember your coach saying 'One last push!', then the next voice you hear is one you're not familiar with, saying 'Clear!' and belonging to a man in a hi-vis jacket holding what appear to be two small electric irons against your chest. Fun, fun, fun.

I've become short of breath just listening to that story.

Some people are addicted to ramp tests. They are the be all and end all; the results to be discussed and picked over with other like-minded sad cases. This sort of person rides up mountains to prepare for ramp tests rather than the other way round. Don't be that guy, Pilgrim. Bike riding takes place outdoors and you go somewhere. OK? Do your hear me, Pilgrim? Do you hear me?

Wh—? Huh? Oh yes, sorry . . . I was just wondering what number I could get on a MAP test.

I don't know why I bother.

Left: *The Wattbike, harbinger of testing times.*

Right: *What was that? VO2 max? That's a kind of shampoo, right?*

R is for Racing

The pinnacle of any man in lycra's racing career isn't a race at all, it's a sportive. It's like a race: you have to plan, enter, train, pay to ride, wear a number and ignore traffic concerns just like the real thing. However, crucially, you don't have to worry about getting left behind. Or how many other people finish in front of you. All you have to do is get round the route. And if that's too hard, there's invariably an easier route. Clever, eh? You can even drive out to whatever remote outpost of civilisation is hosting the event the evening before and stand in the local pub watched by suspicious locals as you sip a half of Guinness with other like-minded individuals.

Of course, Pilgrim, you could actually do a race.

I'm a bit worried about racing, Guide. It all looks a bit scary and competitive, despite all your advice. Everybody I know seems to think that sportives are where the real action is.

OK, well, let's compare the two and give you the tools to do both, OK?

That sounds like a good idea.

I'm full of them, son. Now, let's have a look at the appeal of sportives, or sportifs, or *randonnées* or

audaxes. There are subtle differences between them, but for our purposes they're all much the same: long, challenging, organised rides, where the main object is to complete the course. If you like the idea of the epic ride alloyed with the thrill of being part of an event, but don't need to get the better of your fellow man, these are where you want to be. If you thrive upon competition and the glory of throwing your wheel over the finish line before your rivals, but you don't care that all this action takes place on the perimeter road of an abandoned aerodrome, then you'll lean towards racing.

Is there anything to prevent me doing both?

Not in the slightest, Pilgrim. They require a different attitude though. While taking on a major sportive is a serious undertaking, it's still meant to be fun. If you go to Italy for a sportive, it's still a holiday whichever way you look at it, so take it seriously, but not *too* seriously. I've heard stories of people warming up on turbo trainers in a Butlins car park before a sportive. I think you can guess what the Guide thinks of that, Pilgrim.

Come the revolution, they'll be first up against the wall.

You got it in one. Now, if you decide to take on a race, remember what I told you about the way it's structured. They've inaugurated a fourth category just for beginners, so that's where you'll start. Armed with the Guide's masterclass in bike handling and peloton skills, you should be fully equipped to take on road racing, but unfortunately there are still dangers associated with it, especially at entry level. You see, Pilgrim, not everybody will be as lucky as you to be so well informed in the dark arts of bunch riding. And those tits will likely make some other poor sod fall off before they do.

How do I combat that, Guide?

There are three specific things to remind yourself of. First, the racing tends to be pretty negative. People don't like to stick their noses in the wind. Most guys will want to follow the wheel in front of them and hang in there in the hope that the race will end in a bunch sprint of epic danger that they don't have a cat in hell's chance of winning. As a result, if you ride

Left: *Micco. Not as famous as Wiggo, but celebrated by the stencil man nevertheless.*

Below: *Queue if you want, but there are a thousand ideal gateways and trees between here and the finish.*

at the front, or even get yourself into a little break, you'll be a lot safer and it will be more like real bike racing. Second, you should assume that nobody else knows what they're doing. Not only will this help keep you out of trouble, but when somebody shows a bit of thought or skill it will come as a pleasant surprise. Third, hurry up and win one or two. That's the sure-fire way to ride as few 4th Cat races as possible.

Does it get easier then?

Well, no, of course not. The higher up you go, the faster it gets and the more difficult the parcours. That's wanky talk for route. But it will get safer. There is also the question of what sort of rider you are. At entry level, the courses do tend to be fairly basic circuits, as these are obviously far easier to organise and marshal. Without any major obstacles – I mean hills, not people falling off in front of you – on the route, there are few opportunities for skinny climbers to leave barrel-chested strong guys behind. Therefore, these races favour the sprinters. Even the sort of rider we call a good climber doesn't equate with a professional *grimpeur*. The longest hill you are likely to encounter in British racing is likely to be a mile or maybe two, though granted they can be very steep. The tiny mountain men come into their own on the roads of France, Italy or Spain, where they can spin their tiny gears for an hour or more at a time and leave the heavy boys stuck to the valley bottom. A rider like the great Sean Kelly was thwarted in his designs on Tour de France success by his lack of ability in the high mountains, yet his power took him to the climber's jersey in the Tour of Britain. It's different, that's all.

I don't really know what type of rider I am yet, Guide. I like having a go at anything and everything, but I admit to being a bit scared of the whole racing thing.

Left: *Bradley Wiggins introduces his Sky teammates to the North Downs during the Tour of Britain.*

If safety is your prime concern, maybe you could try time trialling. There will be no other bike rider in sight as you set off at one-minute intervals. The only time you'll get a glimpse of the competition is when somebody goes haring back on the return leg of the course on the other side of the road with a tailwind while you struggle into the gale picking flies out of your clenched teeth. Or you hear that ominous whirring from behind of an approaching disc wheel, and a 60-year-old estate agent with aero helmet, skinsuit and low-profile bike bears down on you.

That sounds much safer.

Yes, much. Except that it takes place on dual carriageways and you can get disqualified for drafting articulated lorries.

Oh, that's choice. Maybe I should stick to the sportives. Some of them have closed roads, so they must be pretty safe.

Closed roads, Pilgrim? Closed to cars, maybe: open to 30,000 middle-aged men in Lycra wobbling along with only 23mm of rubber protecting their hairy knees from meeting gritty tarmacadam. No, that's not closed, and it's certainly not safe. My advice is to find the most attractive sportive, something with a course that you really like the look of, find out the route, then turn up and ride it on any weekend other than the one that the event is on. I always remember with a wry smile a Scottish event that promised its thousands of entrants 'closed roads' in return for a usurious entry fee. I'd found myself by chance on those same roads the week before and seen precisely one car during my Saturday afternoon 100-miler. Somehow, using all my skill and judgement, I managed to avoid colliding with it.

Right: Honister Pass is one of the country's trickiest descents.

Above: The Dragon Ride, one of the UK's biggest sportives, climbs over a lot of South Wales.

Overleaf: Skirting the eastern flank of Cat Bells, south of Keswick.

S is for Socks

One piece of a cyclist's equipment attracts more discussion and thought than any other. Bikes come and go. Frame materials provoke deep disagreement and entrenched views that can lead to battle lines being drawn between otherwise like-minded individuals. The Shimano versus Campagnolo struggle has already outlived the respective companies' founders, and is likely to survive anybody reading this book. Fads in black, white, multi-coloured or neon clothing change from season to season: that's how fashion works. But there is one subject that will arouse strong passions whenever and wherever it is raised. That's right. The sock.

This is the most important part of your training, Pilgrim. In a sense, everything that we have spoken about before now was leading up to this moment. Take a deep breath. Are you ready to talk socks?

I, I think so, Guide. It's a big ask, but I've been preparing for some time. I knew this day would come. It's always been in the back of my mind.

Mine too, Pilgrim, mine too. And I have been a witness to your mental preparation. I have seen the care with which you choose the inner layer of footwear. Now, Pilgrim, you know I am not one to shower praise easily . . .

No kidding.

. . . but it would appear to me that you have grasped the nettle of sock selection and made many good choices already. Well done.

Thank you, Guide. I'm flushed with pride that you've noticed.

All-seeing eye, son. The Guide misses nowt. OK, then, let's take it that we have established that you already have a feel for the importance of the subject and an understanding of what makes a good sock. What we need to do is quantify those impressions, make a hardwired list of dos and don'ts to guide you through the morass of sock choices. If in doubt, just remember the golden rule: WWED.

What would Eddy do?

What would Eddy do. Let me show you the master rocking a sock here back in the late sixties. Just think for a moment about how fashion in general has changed since those days. We're talking *Let It Be* beardy Beatles, the Manson Family, George Best. But look at Eddy Merckx: you could see him riding along the Lower Sunbury Road dressed exactly like that on that day, on this day, or any other day in between and think, that guy is pretty damned cool.

His socks – short, white, thin, ribbed – are the blueprint for any cycling sock. Perfection. Note he shaves his legs, of course, but not his arms. As somebody said to me recently, a man who shaves his legs and his arms probably shaves his vagina too.

What about those shoes though?

Let's give him a break. Those soft, calfskin race slippers were cutting edge at the time. You can't expect him to be shod in something that wasn't going to be invented for another fifteen years or so.

But I digress. Things move on. Let's get back to today's cyclist and the issue of the *chaussettes*. There are a couple of basic moves that we need to discard immediately. The first should be glaringly obvious, but it would appear not to some people: only cycling socks may be used for cycling. Football socks? No. Fluffy sports tube socks? No. Grey work socks? I'm hyperventilating again, Pilgrim.

Take a moment, Guide. I'm with you all the way – cycling socks only. They're thin but comfortable, and they don't wrinkle up inside stiff shoes. There's no question they're the finest tool for the job. But what about length? That's what everybody goes on about.

You're right, Pilgrim. The most contentious of all cycling issues. The reason that sock length is such an emotive subject is that it is hard to find definitive rules that apply in all circumstances. There are two specific factors that can reduce the margins within which it is OK to meddle with one's sock length. I'm going to use a well-known current professional to illustrate my point: Bradley Wiggins.

Here we see him in his pomp during his yellow-draped 2012, swinging through Paris–Nice, the Tour of Romandie, the Critérium du Dauphiné and the

Left: 'Hey! Pilgrim! Look at my socks!'

Right: Brad makes the long black sock his own.

Tour de France itself in leader's jersey after leader's jersey. His sock is longer than the norm without ever suggesting capacity for a shin pad. George Hincapie was a progenitor of the longer sock back in the late nineties, but Brad is taking that to a whole new level with his super-sleek adidas models. These men have two things in common with each other that they don't necessarily share with the majority of cyclists.

Which are?

First, they're tall. Six three and six two respectively, making them both well above average height for a pro scene peopled by little guys. The long sock is an item that should be kept in proportion. These fellows both have a lot more calf to work with than the rest of us, giving them a larger margin. A shorter sock can still work for them – George significantly brought down his high-tide mark over his final few

seasons – but a long sock would demonstrably be a mistake for those of us with less distance between knee and floor. If there's one unbreakable finger-wagging no to be drawn from this, it's that the top of your sock should come nowhere near the underside of your calf muscle.

It's a question of proportion; that makes sound sense. But you said there were two things that George and Brad had going for their ability to make socks work?

Yes, something less quantifiable than height. They've both got it, whether you like them or not. I don't think anybody would disagree. George Clooney's got it. Sean Connery's always had it. Johan Cruyff had it. Socrates had it in spades – the footballer, not the philosopher. And David Bowie could sell tuition in it.

Huh? What have they got to do with cycling socks?

Nothing. Or everything, depending on your viewpoint, Pilgrim. What they've all undeniably but unquantifiably got is cool. Dripping out of them. And if you're cool, you can smoke fags while warming up to come on as a sub. You can advertise coffee machines. You can wear an obvious toupée. You can do all of these things without losing your *je ne sais quoi*. And what's more, you can wear long black socks with white shoes. That's what you can do if you're cool like these fellows.

Do you have an opinion on sock colour, Guide?

My answer may surprise you, Pilgrim: no, not really. White socks with black shoes, *à la* Cav, is very suave and traditional, but it's also a bit seventies Second Division footballer. Coloured socks were a nineties phenomenon that stuck. I can picture Gewiss riders shooting effortlessly clear of the professional peloton in a haze of questionable substances and pale blue socks. By the twenty-first century, teams were actually designing socks in patterns to match the rest of the team strip to no great detriment of their overall performance. The closest we can get to a colour crime in the sock department is the black sock/white shoe combo we touched on earlier, and we've established that the coolest riders can carry that off. Coloured socks are here to stay.

So, to sum up, your socks can be any colour, the height must be commensurate to the length of your leg, and you can wear more outlandish concoctions if you're tall and cool.

Nicely zeitgeisted, Pilgrim. If you're short and uncool, stick to the straightforward. If only Cadel Evans had put himself in my hands.

Left: *Who doesn't dream of pulling on new socks for every single bike ride?*   **Right:** *Oh, Cadel. Where do I start?*

T is for Technology

The key to really utilising technology is to choose the best bit, and stick to it. Power meter, heart-rate monitor, milometer or GPS? Either go for something that combines the lot, or pick one and one alone.

Those are your handlebars, not your computlebars; you need room to put your hands on them. It's all bollocks anyway.

There's a lot of it about, eh?

A lot of what about, Guide?

All this technology stuff. Information and measurement flying about. For the cyclist, is it a boon or a curse?

It's nice to know how far you've been or how fast you're going.

As long as it's good news, yes. You're not so keen on knowing what little distance you've covered or how slow you're going, I'll wager. And Twitter

and Facebook are rattling with stories about how some idiot rode at full pelt into the back of a UPS van outside their house while trying to set a Strava personal best. Let's have a sift through the technology available to you, Pilgrim. See if we can separate what delivers true advantage and what should be dragged across your home screen to the Recycle Bin.

What did they use in the old days, Guide? What did Merckx use?

Big Ted's on-bike use of technology extended to a battery-powered electric shaver to run over his calves on the start line. He would never be far from a spirit level and spanner to ensure his saddle was bang on either, but if we're calling that technology, we may as well start talking about how Neolithic man moved them stones from Pembrokeshire to Wiltshire. I think we have to agree that some form of electric power needs to be involved before we call any of these cycling aids technology. Electricity or, as my nan called it, witchcraft. God knows what she would have made of a Wii.

When did computers first come in?

The Avocet cycling computer, a particularly neat little gem available in a rainbow of colours, was widely spread across the handlebars of the eighties. Small and neat with nice big numbers on its screen, it told you how fast you were going and how far you'd been. Many disapproved instantly – remember that maxim about distance being measured only by time spent in the saddle – but it was grudgingly accepted as useful. Many more would argue that all subsequent developments have been spurious.

What else do people want to measure?

If you're interested in where you've been or where you're going, the GPS has been a handy add-on. Dead useful for mountain bikers adrift in the middle of nowhere too. A good one can also measure speed and distance without recourse to magnets and sensors on your wheel and forks. Let's be honest though, the vast majority of us spend our days rolling along the same roads we always ride on, so that's of limited usefulness. What people really want to measure, both as a training aid and a preening aid, is their own performance and how it is hopefully improving.

Now we're talking. Heart rate, power output, that sort of thing?

Yep. Heart rate was the first big thing. The cyclists, runners, swimmers, triathletes, weightlifters – God, chess players for all I know – of the nineties relied

on heart-rate monitors, usually in the form of a wristwatch and a band around your chest. It was a useful tool to see how you were doing. You'd work out what your absolute maximum BPM was, and then discover your 'threshold' as a percentage of that number. By training on or around that threshold, where you go from sustainable aerobic energy expenditure into short-lived anaerobic bursts, you could improve your fitness and ability.

That sounds great. What's wrong with that?

Nothing really, it just wasn't particularly reliable. Some days you'd feel shit. Some days you'd feel great, but the heart rate didn't really want to rise for some reason. At worst, the heart rate monitor was a very arbitrary way of setting programmes and targets, and experienced riders and coaches have always taken heart rate readings as handy information, but dosed with a liberal sprinkling of salt.

But power output readings are more accurate?

At the end of the day, once we know your weight and the terrain, it will take a finite amount of power to drive your bicycle along at a certain speed. So, yes, power output measuring is more useful in terms of judging where you are fitness-wise and in setting training goals, especially if you're preparing for a difficult event. Accurate recording of power output has traditionally been difficult and expensive, mainly the province of the fabled SRM cranks that were pioneered by Greg LeMond, but more recently splattered lavishly across Team GB machines. It's easier and marginally cheaper to do it now with groovy gadgets like Vector pedals and Stages cranks replacing your normal components with power-measuring equipment. It's still important to remember that when it comes down to the real

Right: If you have an altimeter on your computer, Hartside Top on the Pennines will give you a decent elevation of 1,904 feet above sea level.

thing, you've got to just bury yourself sometimes. Hills like the Koppenberg or Ventoux are no respecters of technology or power meters. They rate you in terms of sweat, endeavour and ability. Never forget that, Pilgrim.

I am suitably chastened, Guide.

Now, the key equation for all those interested in getting the best out of themselves is your power-to-weight ratio. This is usually measured in watts per kilo. This is a much maligned methodology, as it is at the heart of Lance Armstrong and Dr Ferrari's drug-assisted performance programme, but it remains true that the maths is good, whether you cheat to get there or not. Ferrari maintained that if a rider can knock out 6.7 watts of power for every kilo of weight, he can win the Tour de France. So you can see that low body weight is just as important as strength. If you can get skinny without getting weak, you will fulfil your potential as a cyclist.

Would those figures alter depending on the terrain though?

Yes, for sure. That's why Alberto Contador and Chris Froome win Grand Tours, Tom Boonen and Fabian Cancellara win classics, and Mark Cavendish wins sprints. In fact, Team Sky deliberately prepared the eventual winner Bradley Wiggins to come into the 2012 Tour de France a few kilos heavier than the year before. The route had more time-trialling miles and less high mountain stage finishes, meaning he would benefit from a little more power without being penalised for the extra weight. Cycling is a horses for courses game, Pilgrim; you know that by now.

Left: *Autumn on Netley Heath, covered by the Olympic peloton at London 2012.*

True, Guide. And horses don't win both the Derby and the Grand National, do they?

By Jove, I think he's got it.

So, that's all these training aids and assistances covered. Can we talk about Strava?

Jesus. I knew it. It was all going so well. He lulls me into a false sense of security by demonstrating his understanding of my methods and then sucker punches me when I'm looking the other way. Strava. If there's one thing that's guaranteed to get my veins up to a sensible cooking temperature, it's Strava. OK, OK, calm . . . let me take a deep breath and address the demon known as Strava in a rational, sensible way.

I'm sorry, Guide. I didn't mean to upset you, it's just . . .

I know, son, I know. Don't worry. Everybody loves Strava. It's not just you. It's important to cover it. I just don't like it. Right, then, putting my personal antipathy to one side, Strava is a remarkable twenty-first-century phenomenon. Effectively an online GPS-driven database where everybody who taps into the Strava diaspora can compare their performance to everybody else on there. Sounds harmless and entertaining.

And a useful training assistant, according to my friends?

Well, I suppose it can be. As well as looking at how everybody else is doing, you can compare your current performances over a regular ride to your past results, seeing if there is any improvement. If only it stayed as simple as that. What one gets instead is a plethora of petty, childish, internecine messing around, as people try to better each other. While this is commendable and understandable over such accepted courses as the aforementioned Koppenberg and Ventoux, or even more parochial targets like the Horseshoe Pass or even Box Hill, it doesn't stop there, does it? People claim

bragging rights for being the fastest between the bus stop at the end of their cul-de-sac and their garage door. Crazies even boast about making the fastest descent of twisting, single-track Devon lanes that can hide a Massey Ferguson or a John Deere around every corner. Madness. Strava stops being a tool or a diversion for these guys and becomes their entire *raison d'être*. They live to ride, but they ride to Strava.

It does sound a little bit tragic when you put it like that.

Not just tragic, Pilgrim, but rife with abuse. If you ever go for a group ride with people using Strava, be prepared for them to trundle along the lanes at a creeping pace, never for once sticking their noses in the wind, preparing above all else for the one little hill you're all going to tackle. Then they're off the front like a bullet out of a barrel, flying up the gradient like Ayrton Senna towards a brick wall, only to collapse in a heap at the top, PB proudly set. Wankers. That, Pilgrim, is not a real performance. Likewise, I heard tell recently of a lad who set an amazing time on the historic climb up to the Madonna del Ghisallo high above Lake Como. His friends battered themselves for the rest of their little cycling trip in their efforts to beat his mark – all doomed to failure. Not that surprising; he finally confessed on the way home that he'd actually been up it on the bus.

Right: *If it's still bleeping, I must still be alive.*

U is for Unlucky

Most unlucky instances on the bike involve an unscheduled human/tarmac interface. Don't be tempted to weep like a small child, either in genuine pain or because you've scratched your rear mech. Get up, not too quickly, but stoically and accepting of the inevitability of these occasional distractions, quickly check your bike for genuine damage that may affect its ability to carry you home, and ignore any blood. Pretend you haven't even noticed. Continue as if this is all part and parcel of being a pro, stop at the café even and talk about other things until you get home. Then run a bath, gingerly strip off your tattered clothes and have a good, long cry.

Have you fallen off your bike yet, Pilgrim?

Yes. Yes, I have, Guide. I'm ashamed, but I have fallen off my bike.

Hush, man, dry those tears. Falling off is part of cycling. Everybody crashes sometimes. The trick is to crash as rarely as possible and to do it without dying.

I was kind of banking on that.

Good. Keep it up. Now, if I can ask a delicate question: did you crash because you didn't click out of your pedals?

Oh God. Yes, I fell off because I forgot I was clipped into my pedals and toppled over at a set of traffic lights in front of a large number of people, most of whom drove round me laughing and pointing. I hope you're happy. I wasn't expecting the Spanish Inquisition.

Nobody expects the Inquisition, Pilgrim. Again, try not to get too upset; everybody does it. Well, I say everybody, obviously I haven't done it. It's people like you, Pilgrim, who topple over at the lights. OK, you're excused one. Just one tiny topple. Fall off at the lights on more than one occasion and you will be drummed out of our secret society.

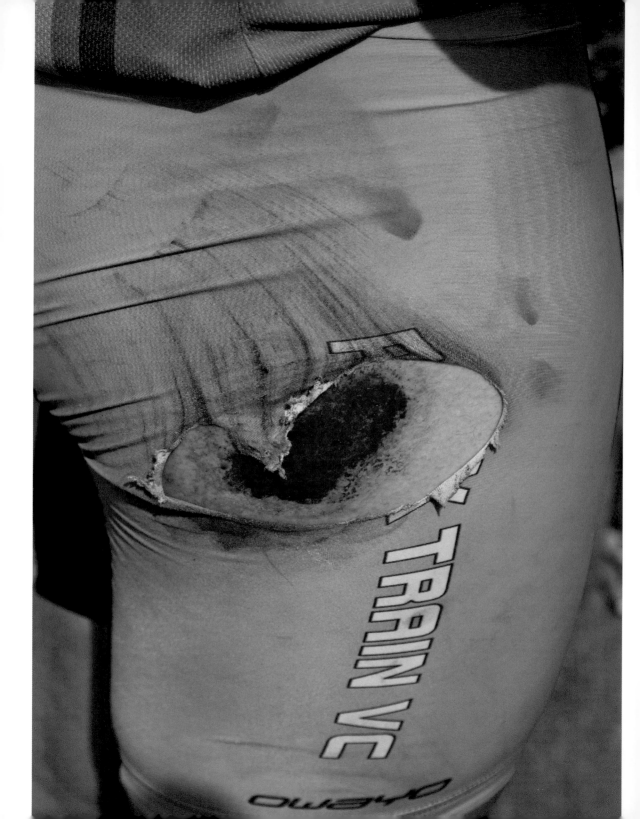

I didn't know I was in a secret society.

That's because it's secret. Now, listen carefully. I'm going to deliver the Guide's instructions on the safe use of clipless pedals. They were originally known as safety pedals, much to the consternation of the twenty-first-century newcomer to cycling. This is because old racing pedals with clips and straps weren't just awkward to get into – the former GB road race champion Matt Stephens got dropped in the first 50 yards of a road race once while trying to get his foot into the pedal – it was because once you were in, you were in. There was a cleat with a lateral groove cut into it under the ball of your foot on old-style race shoes. That groove would slot over the raised trailing edge of traditional racing pedals and you would pull your toe strap up tight to secure it. Nothing short of an improvised explosive device at the roadside could remove your foot from that contraption. Then, a French company who made ski equipment, Look, made a version of their pop-out sprung ski bindings for cycling, and the clipless pedal was born.

I can see it's an improvement.

But how to stop falling off while mastering the clipless pedal, Pilgrim, that's the question, eh? There are three things to remember. First, clip out before you need to, not when you need to. Don't wait till you get to the junction. Better to clip out needlessly than be unable to twist your foot out at the last moment. Second, don't try to twist out when your foot is at the top of its revolution. There's less leverage there; much easier to flick your ankle outward when your leg is straight down. Third, and this is where most people come unstuck, make sure you clip out of the correct side. Clipping out of the left pedal as you wobble towards your right is the number one cause of clipless pedal embarrassment. There is some nasty law of physics which dictates that it is impossible to clip out once the toppling has begun. Practise on grass for a soft landing. Turf, I mean. Drugs and bike riding don't mix. Ah, wait, I need to rephrase that.

Left: *Ouch. At least you won't have to wear those shorts again.*

Below: *Ouch. I forgot the Sudocrem this morning.*

It's OK, Guide. I know what you mean. Do some people crash more than others?

Unquestionably. Some people are just lacking skills in the bike handling area. The nineties Swiss perennial Grand Tour contender Alex Zülle springs to mind. He would probably have been capable of crashing off the sofa while watching *X Factor*. There are others that crash regularly but it's never their fault. These guys are probably just not reactive enough to avoid their Zülle-like pals. Then there are the Mark Cavendishes of this world. They're just not scared of crashing, so they do. One thing tends to link them all though: myopia. If you need glasses or contacts, make sure the ones you use for cycling are as good as you can get.

Any other tips?

You can learn a lot from mountain biking and mountain bikers, who, of course, are always falling off. It will teach you that you can fall off without it being disastrous. OK, you're likely to get a softer landing in a muddy forest, but the concept of crashing being part of what you do is worth embracing. Practical things you can learn from the off-road weekend warriors and adapt to road biking are rife. My favourite maxim, which I heard years ago, is 'If you look at it, you hit it'. Don't look at obstacles on the trail or the road, look at the path you want to take to avoid it and your bike will naturally follow. It's like a cricketer needing to get his head in line with the ball to be able to hit through it cleanly. In fact, let's send the England cricket team mountain biking. Some may improve their game and others may have their careers ended. Either way, we win as a country.

You need to be more careful in the wet, of course.

Left: *A Basque rider shows his natural prowess for Flandrian cobbles on the Oude Kwaremont.*

Naturally, Pilgrim, but the saving grace is that one tends to slide when one hits a wet surface rather than stick and rip as can be the case on dry roads. Always wear mitts or gloves. You might think you're cool or hard to ride without them, but you're neither Tom Boonen nor Sean Yates. The palm of your hand is usually the first piece of you to hit the ground, and as well as cushioning your hand on the bars during your ride, the mitt will help you survive a sudden and unexpected end to that ride.

How about traffic?

Unquestionably the most dangerous thing about cycling. Let's talk strategy in dealing with motorists. The first thing is to get away from the tribalism that affects all of us at times: bloody motorists, bloody cyclists, bloody pedestrians. A lot of motorists are cyclists, most cyclists are motorists, and virtually all of us are pedestrians. Personifying the battle takes away its dangerous edge, so meet the eyes of motorists, smile, thank them unnecessarily. They're much less likely to knock off a fellow human being than a bloody cyclist. I know that justice is on the side of the cyclist more often than not in altercations between car and bike, but there is little righteous satisfaction in the motorist getting three points on his licence when you've just flatlined on your life support machine.

Fitting in with the traffic is the safest way to ride?

Correct. Bumping along in the gutter invites cars to ignore you as road furniture. In normal town traffic, your speed won't be that different to the cars, so ride like you're driving. Other road users will treat you with a little more respect, and you can reinforce that respect by stopping at traffic lights, not hopping on to pavements or riding the wrong way up one-way streets. A great tip I picked up from a cycle safety trainer once – I thought I already

knew everything but, she showed me a few things, I can tell you – is your positioning on the road. We instinctively know that if you ride too close to the kerb, cars will come too close to you. This is because, she explained, the motorist visualises the space between the car and the kerb with you in the centre of it. Ride four feet out from the gutter and the driver will subconsciously give you another four feet of breathing space. Ride six inches out and you're asking to get your backside tickled by a wing mirror.

Who is the unluckiest cyclist of all time?

Ah, that's easy. Raymond Poulidor. He was never going to be the luckiest – his nickname was Poupou, for God's sake – but he was adored by the French public in the sixties and seventies who would wait each year to see how he would mess up his chances of winning the Tour. He rode fourteen Tours de France, finished on the podium in Paris no fewer than eight times, yet never, ever wore the yellow jersey. Not even for a day. To put that in perspective, Lance Armstrong stood on the same number of Tour podiums as Poupou, but he spent 83 days in yellow. Poupou came up with a never-ending list of unlucky reasons for losing the Tour, usually to Jacques Anquetil or Eddy Merckx: crashes, illness, that sort of thing. My favourite is in 1964 when he finished second to Anquetil by 55 seconds after failing to drop him in an epic head-to-head battle on the Puy-de-Dôme.

That's not exactly unlucky though, is it?

No, not at all. But what they don't tell you is that he'd already lost two minutes earlier in the race when he got a wheel change and his mechanic, trying to give him the traditional push back into the action, actually pushed him off and his bike broke. Now that *is* unlucky.

Left: Hey, you ride through the pile of leaves first. Then you'll hit the hidden dog turd.

V is for Vulcanised

Tyre selection is a massive test of your cool. For instance, practicality would suggest that a hard, puncture-resistant tyre with reddish-brown side walls would be a good idea for bowling around the lanes of a weekend. After all, the last thing you want is for everybody to stand there shivering and watching while you struggle ham-fistedly to get a tyre lever under your lightweight rubber to fix a hole. The extra rolling resistance of this bombproof tyre will even help you train, requiring as it does a little more power to turn it over on those heavy roads. But if we were practical people, we wouldn't be here, would we? We'd be doing something useful, like gardening, or earning money, or helping our kids with their maths homework. So let's put the most expensive, temperamental silky strips of latex on our unsuitably flimsy wheels.

To paraphrase the greatest music ensemble of the twentieth century: wheels can take you around but wheels can also cut you down. Geddy, Alex and Neil told us that on the closing track of the mid-period Rush album, *Grace Under Pressure*. Neil Peart is in fact an accomplished bike rider, going so far as to have had the band's tour dates arranged to enable him to ride between cities and take a full-time bike roadie as part of their crew. Hey, that's another kind of roadie. Funny.

Who are Rush?

Who are Rush? Are you serious, Pilgrim? I . . . I'm momentarily lost for words. And saddened.

I'm sorry, Guide. I just don't really know much about music.

Ah, OK. Wait. Just wait a second. You don't know much about music because you're committed to the bike, right, Pilgrim? Devoted to the way, the truth, the light. No time for anything else. Is that right?

Well, I suppose you could say that. I would probably rather . . .

I can only handle your ignorance if I offset it against your dedication, Pilgrim, so I will say that and be done with it. Anyway, the point that Geddy, Alex, Neil and I were making, if admittedly in a pretty trite and

hammy way that does their reputation as decades-spanning chroniclers of the human condition no favours whatsoever, is that wheels are important. And very important if you get them wrong. Your wheel and tyre choice can make the difference between a deeply satisfying ride and a disaster of King Lot proportions.

When I go into bike shops, I look at the bikes, then the clothes, then the wheels. That's a reckoning of how sexy they are, I think.

Wheels: third sexiest thing in cycling. Not bad, Pilgrim, not bad. I don't think I'm going to disagree with you there. So, to get to the nub of what makes a good wheel – we'll come to tyres when we've got the hardware sorted – we need to look at what properties it needs to have. It's often said that turning weight is more important than stationary weight, meaning that saving weight on your wheels and tyres is more important than saving it elsewhere on your bike. Why? Because you expend effort to get it spinning as well as to propel it along the road, so lighter wheels equal less effort and greater acceleration. After weight, we value rigidity, strength, comfort and aerodynamic profile in our wheels. The trick is to get the right blend for the application.

That's why people have different wheels for the same bike?

Exactly, Pilgrim. The most obvious example is training wheels. And, for our American friends, training wheels are the wheels you ride on when you're training, not the noisy little plastic outriders on toddlers' bikes. They're stabilisers. Training wheels need to be strong, reliable and cheap. We put them on for crud-covered winter roads and batter them until the spring sunshine comes out and we lovingly refit some carbon beauties.

And you don't use the same wheels for time trials as road racing, do you?

No, the needs of the different disciplines ask different questions of your wheels. In time trialling, acceleration and weight are rarely as important as they are in road racing. Once you're out of the hutch, you want to settle into your top speed quickly and stay there. You need rigidity to ensure that you're delivering all the power you can muster and you need aerodynamics to

Above: *Soft rubber rides nicer but punctures quicker.*

Right: *Suits you, sir. How many would you like?*

cut through the wind. Hence the ideal time-trial wheel set-up is a solid carbon disc on the back and a deep-sectioned carbon wheel on the front.

Why not a disc wheel on the front too?

It's been tried. In fact, it was very popular in the late eighties after Francesco Moser used a low-profile bike and two discs to beat Eddy Merckx's hour record, but handling was always tricky, especially if there was a crosswind. When people started using tri-bars as well, in 1989, it was virtually impossible to hold your bike in a straight line with a disc on the front, so you now usually only see them in Graham Watson's old Tour de France pictures of Bernard Hinault or Laurent Fignon.

But there are variations of wheel for road racing too?

There sure are. Climbers will often have super-light wheels for the mountains, weighing as little as 900 grammes a pair. However, these won't make everyone climb better. The low body weight of the true climber means that he will generate less torque than a man of more average build, and the heavier rider would be better served in sacrificing a little of that low weight for a bit more rigidity to better utilise his increased power. Riders interested in escaping the bunch and riding solo or in a small group tend to prefer deep section wheels for their increased aerodynamic properties. While I think of it, Pilgrim, always remember that aerodynamics only become important when you're already going quickly. There's a performance delta, an exponential growth in usefulness in aerodynamics at high speed. You don't need to worry about your shape when you're struggling up Holme Moss at 10mph. However, the profile you and your bike offer to the wind at 30mph on a dual carriageway has an enormous effect on your speed.

Left: The right tyres for the right roads. Horses for courses.

You mentioned comfort too?

Yes. Not just for the obvious reasons of saving your arse as much punishment as possible on a long ride. Bumpy roads or cobbles need some absorption if you're going to come off those sections near the front. The rough stuff doesn't just mess you up, it slows you down, so you need your wheels to take some sting out if you're going to remain competitive.

Right. Well, it seems I need a wall-mounted wheel rack to keep the beautiful collection I've been mentally accruing during this conversation. What tyres am I going to put on them all?

Tyres have become a little wider in the last few years. It was always intuitively felt that the narrower your tyre, the less resistance, and the quicker you'd roll. Sounds sensible, eh? It's not wrong, but tests proved that once your tyre got to below about 23mm it just didn't make much difference, and it's hard to make a wheel that's up to the rigours of the road but is narrower than that, so, as a rule, they don't bother. In fact, the extra comfort and grip you get from a slightly wider tyre, say 25mm, will often outweigh the tiny amount of extra resistance. Just don't forget to check that they'll fit in your bike before you splash out on expensive rubber. Some race frames have such tight clearances that anything bigger than a 23mm will catch under your brakes or fizz against your seat tube.

Do I need tread on my tyres? I get a bit nervous on wet roads and slick tyres.

A common worry, Pilgrim, but entirely unwarranted. Tread doesn't give you grip. Tread is designed to divert water away from a big car tyre to allow the rubber to make contact with the road. When you've only got 23mm between you and the tarmac, you want as much of it as possible on the deck. Tread comes in handy when you need to take a hold on rough surfaces, like riding a cross bike or a mountain bike, but, counter-intuitively, tread is sketchy on greasy tarmac. There's still a bit of a friend's face on the corner outside the Odeon when he leant over a bit too far in November, forgetting he was on his cross bike.

Ouch. What about tubulars?

A lot of folk, young 'uns usually, are scared of tubs. A tyre that's glued on to a rim rather than hooked on with an inner tube inside frightens them. First, they think it might come unstuck – it won't if you get a pro to put it on – but mainly they panic about getting a puncture. In actual fact, it's at least as quick and easy to change a tub out on a ride as a tube. You just rip the buggered one off, and stretch an old one round. The remnants of tub cement on the tyre and the rim will hold it in place if you refrain from doing anything too stupid. Just don't, whatever you do, have a brand new tub as your spare. Stretching a new tub onto a rim is a hell of a job. Keep your old ones when they're looking a bit tired – ha! – and carry one under your saddle, lashed on with a leather toe strap. Old school.

Tubulars aren't the same as tubeless, are they?

Tubeless. No, they're an irritating modern invention that their users, like TV evangelists, will tell you are miles better than tubs or 'clinchers', as we call tyres with inner tubes. I've ridden them. They felt exactly the same except a bit heavier – you save the weight of the inner tube, but the tyre is heavier and you have to fill it with noxious goo – and when you do get a puncture, the stuff goes absolutely everywhere. I'll have my old tyres back, thanks.

That's been highly informative, Guide. Just one more thing. That guy who fell off outside the Odeon? That was you, wasn't it?

Might've been.

Below: *If the correct number of bikes to own is one more than you have, how many wheels can your house handle?*

Right: *If you have wheels for sprinting and wheels for climbing, which wheels do you sprint uphill on?*

W is for Winter

Oof. Parky out there, eh? Who'd want to go out in this? Madness.

I'll tell you who: someone who spends all his spare time and money on lovely cycling kit. When it's cold, our eyes light up. An opportunity to put everything on at once. Beautifully tailored, technically implacable layer upon layer. I bought these camel-lined polar bear-skin overshoes specifically for days like this, so long may they last. Now all we need is a café with an Aga and we're laughing. Cooking on gas, you might say.

What is the most expensive bit of kit you own, Pilgrim, apart from your bike and shoes?

Hmm … that would be a fantastic Castelli thermal jacket I bought in the sale at the end of last winter. I've been waiting all year to wear it.

Exactly. There's more going on in winter kit: more material, more technology involved in keeping you warm and dry. It's bound to be expensive. And we love to wear expensive kit, don't we?

We sure do.

Those luxurious gloves. Those beautiful overshoes. That silky under-helmet skullcap. That toasty undervest.

The hot-water bottle Mummy prepares for me every night.

Eh?

Ah, nothing.

So there's plenty of good motivation to get us out there and ride away those winter mornings. But what about the long, dark nights of the soul that

are December and January evenings? Not much fun riding in the dark, is it, Pilgrim? What are you going to do then?

It'll be good to get some return on those lights I bought. Eye-watering in more ways than one, they were.

Yes, good call. Get out there, show everybody else who's boss. You're out there doing it while they're stuck inside. Of course, just because they're stuck inside doesn't have to mean they're not riding their bikes, does it?

Oh, I see. You're talking about turbos?

That's right, Pilgrim: turbos, indoor trainers, static bikes, rollers. Derided as boring by many cyclists, but actually a great way to get you through those long nights and deliver you like a speeding bullet into the March sunshine when the clocks leap forward. There are a whole lot of tricks to make indoor training fun. Let's start with the turbo trainer. These come in a breathtaking array of models these days, so it's worth weighing up which one will be right for you.

I've been reading about turbos. You can get wind ones, magnetic ones and fluid ones. What's all that about?

OK. Back in the day, all turbo trainers were wind powered. You clamped your back wheel onto a metal roller that spun a fan. As you pedalled away, the blades of the fan provided the resistance to make pedalling hard enough to make the whole thing work. The drawback was the lack of adjustability and the incredible noise. It was a bit like somebody revving up a Mini Metro in your living room. The rest of us were delighted when similar devices were invented that used fluid or magnetism to provide the requisite resistance. Much quieter, they also tend to feel a little more realistic; you pedal circles a little more naturally than stomping up and down. They're adjustable too, though I have to say that you can adjust the resistance perfectly adequately by changing gear anyway.

So how do you make it more interesting?

Well, after you get past the basic turbo features, they go up in price depending on the extras available, so if

you like facts and figures about your ride, or want to follow a programme – the machine will automatically adjust the resistance – the more advanced models are for you. You can go right up to virtual reality type things that will enable you to ride alongside other lonely types across the globe. Ride up Alpe d'Huez with your virtual friends, who are probably called artie_fufkin or braindriller5, all from the comfort of your own draughty garage.

I think I'll set mine up indoors.

Ah, very wise, Pilgrim. In that case, a world of possibilities opens up for you. Get a big telly and a quiet turbo, and the world is your lobster.

I can watch films and train at the same time!

You could indeed decide to work your way through the back catalogue of Akira Kurosawa or Danny Kaye, but you will come up against the other problem that confronts the long-term turbo user. If you're on it for an hour or more, it's not just the brain that will need stimulating back into life. Your biffin's bridge will be feeling the pinch.

Sorry? Did you say biffin's bridge? What's that?

You know, Pilgrim. Your biffin's bridge. Your schacht. Your gooch. Your, err, gusset region. Basically, after an hour your bollocks will be as numb as Piers Morgan's sense of humility. Turbo riding puts more weight on the saddle region than the real thing, and the repetitive nature of plugging away without ups and downs in the road or traffic lights to give you a break will leave your tackle feeling like it's been cryogenically stored. That's why we need to find ways of jazzing up the action a bit. Give your boys a break and add some quality to your training at the same time.

Left: *In cold weather, everything warms up … except your feet. They just get colder and colder. It's science.*

Right: *With pitches at 30%, Hardknott Pass vies for the title of Britain's steepest road.*

RACE UPDATE
STAGE 4 · 148.5km

ADELAIDE, SOUTH AUSTRALIA

Crikey. Not all plain sailing, then.

No. If you've got the turbo indoors, get some cycling on the telly. Imagine you're in the pack and react when they react: hills, sprints and so on. You can actually buy videos that use real clips put together to get you making an effort, but with a little imagination you can do it yourself. If you've got a big enough living room, get a couple of mates round and line yourselves up in front of the screen. That's about as social as a social ride can get. I promise you'll have fun.

Let's suppose, just for a moment, just for the sake of argument, that I don't have a supply of pals who want to come turbo training at my house. Just suppose . . .

Understood, Pilgrim. Fair enough, if you – no, let's say if somebody you know – is training in front of the TV on their own, plan ahead and record some live football from the weekend or the Champions League. You need a live game, because you can use the clock in the corner of the screen to see how you're doing. Now, once you've warmed up – say, ten minutes steady – keep an eye on the ref. As I was saying earlier, every time he blows the whistle, or the ball goes out, drop a cog or two and pedal like billy-o until it happens again. If you do this for the whole game, you've got two 45-minute interval sessions with a gap in the middle to rehydrate properly. You sweat buckets indoors.

Does it work with rugby too?

In theory, yes, but in practice the man in the middle blows his whistle every other breath and the steroid-bound public school thugs are trying to kick the egg into Row Z at every opportunity. Try it, by all means, but you'll find that you don't know if you're

coming or going. Mind you, that may be preferable to watching Barcelona. You'll be pleading for somebody to hoof it into touch when they string 40 passes together in one move.

I suppose that rehydration thing is still important indoors.

Yes, even more than usual. But it's not just you who needs protection from sweating too much; your bike needs it too. Once you've warmed up, it'll drip out of every pore. Every bike shop will tell you tales that begin with a guy saying 'My computer's not working', before presenting a bike that is entirely encrusted with a solid layer of man salt. Don't let that be you, Pilgrim.

A towel over the front of your bike won't just give you something to wipe your face on occasionally, it will save your beloved machine from looking like the set of *Raise the Titanic*.

OK, that's turbo trainers. What's the story with rollers?

Ah, the purist's training. You wouldn't catch Eddy Merckx on a turbo. You plonk your rear wheel on the two rollers at the back, your front wheel on the other one that's joined to the rear ones by a belt, hop on and ride off. All in the comfort of your own living room.

Wow. You just ride and balance? What happens if you fall off?

You hope that you don't entirely destroy the comfort of your own living room, which is eminently possible. That's the danger and the beauty of the rollers: it's real bike riding indoors, with all the pleasures and pitfalls that implies. Of course, there is something else you could do to get you through the winter.

What's that?

Take up skiing and piss off.

Left: *Rollers and a 55-inch television? Check your home and contents insurance first.*

Overleaf: *The Dolomites are home to some of the world's finest cycling roads.*

X is for Existentialism

As Rush once said, answering their own questions: why are we here? Because we're here. Why does it happen? Because it happens.

Or, to paraphrase Alfie, if you ain't got your peace of mind, you ain't got nothing. If they ain't got you one way, they've got you another. What's it all about? Know what I mean?

So, Pilgrim, I got a text from my friend Bruce on the 30th of December. He was away in Australia.

Nice. Was he on holiday? Texting to wish you a Happy New Year because they're twelve hours ahead or something?

No, he wasn't really on holiday, and he was keen to let me know he was texting me a day before New Year's Eve. He wanted me to know that he'd managed to get something done with a whole day to spare.

Oh really? What was that?

Over the preceding 364 days of the year leading up to his text he had ridden, according to his bike computer, 40,000 kilometres.

That's mind-blowing. Hang on a minute . . . let me just . . . there's a calculator on here somewhere . . . No way. That's more than 100 a day.

Yes, it is. Though not the world record for distance ridden in a year. You know how they used to say that Bob Beamon's world record long jump would never be beaten? He flew through the thin air of Mexico City at the 1968 Olympics and soared for nearly 30 feet – almost two feet further than anybody had ever

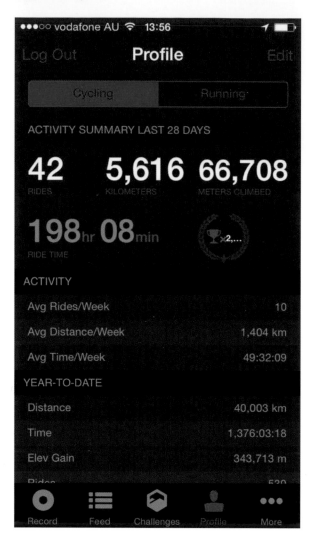

●●●○○ vodafone AU 📶 13:56 📶 🔋

Log Out **Profile** Edit

Cycling · Running

ACTIVITY SUMMARY LAST 28 DAYS

42 **5,616** **66,708**
RIDES   KILOMETERS   METERS CLIMBED

198hr **08**min 🏆×2,...
RIDE TIME

ACTIVITY

Avg Rides/Week	10
Avg Distance/Week	1,404 km
Avg Time/Week	49:32:09

YEAR-TO-DATE

Distance	40,003 km
Time	1,376:03:18
Elev Gain	343,713 m
Rides	530

⦿ ☰ ⬗ 👤 •••
Record   Feed   Challenges   Profile   More

Above: Year to date, 40,003 kilometres. That deserves a big slice of cake.

Right: Solo miles give you time to think.

jumped before. It was beaten eventually though, by two inches, in 1991 by Mike Powell, which is still the record. That's two of the longest-held world records in sport. Impressive, huh?

Err, yes, but what's the connection?

What indeed, Pilgrim. Have you heard of Tommy Godwin, Pilgrim? No? He was born in Stoke on Trent. In the calendar year of 1939, Tommy rode 120,805 kilometres. That's 75,065 miles. Now, that's what I call a long-held world record. If Bruce wants to take Tommy Godwin's world record, he'll have to ride three times as far next year as he did last year. Doesn't seem possible, does it? What's more, he won't even get in the *Guinness Book of Records* if he does it. The successors to the McWhirter twins deem it 'too dangerous'.

It's hard getting your head round those figures, Guide.

It's getting your head round stuff that I want to talk about, Pilgrim. You know what Bruce and the late Tommy Godwin share, apart from very, very sore arses? The ability to focus their minds on a target. To exploit the singular nature of the individual to find meaning in a meaningless world. To rise above the disorientation and confusion that follows when one realises that this is all there is. No grand plan. No supreme being charting your course. You've got to get out there and do it yourself.

I see, I think.

Do you, Pilgrim? Existence precedes essence, Pilgrim. It's about who you are, not what you are. You can't define your true self by saying you're Welsh, or that you're a farmer, or a policeman, or by what school you went to. That's merely your essence. Your existence is you. You're here. I can see you here in front of me. You control your own being, your movements, your path.

All right, you really have lost me now.

Kierkegaard told us that life is not a problem to be solved, but a reality to be experienced. He's telling you to get out there, Pilgrim. He would have made a bloody good cyclist. These are the realities of existence for you to wrestle with when you're out there alone on the long and lonely road.

It is really just like my ex-girlfriend said, then. It really is all about me, all the time.

I don't really think she had Kierkegaard in mind, Pilgrim. She was just moaning that you were out on your bike all the time when she was trying to get shit done on her own. You pissed her off, and now you're paying the price by ploughing your lonely furrow, just

like Tommy Godwin. I'm trying to show you that, in this absurd world, you need to make your own way and create your own meaning. Tommy knew that. To dare is to lose your footing for a moment. Not to dare is just losing.

Kierkegaard again?

Yep. I want you to keep these thoughts with you when you're out on your bike on those terrible days, Pilgrim, when your mates failed to turn up, but you were there in the rain. Think of Tommy, knowing that if he missed a day, that was 300 kilometres he'd have to find somewhere else. He intuitively knew, like Kierkegaard, that the highest things in life are not to

be heard about, read about or seen, but are to be lived. Commitment is an act, not a word. That last one's Sartre, by the way.

Oh, I know him. He said that hell is other people. Which is something I'm beginning to realise. Look, I've really got to get on ...

What is happiness but the simple harmony that exists between man and the life that he leads? That was Camus, philosopher and goalkeeper. He must have known a fair bit about disappointment. The number of times he stood alone near the penalty spot having picked the ball out of the net and then been left to think about it. No wonder he came out with some good stuff.

I don't understand what this is all about.

It's not meant to be easy, son. These long hours of dedication and contemplation can bring some understanding, but you must always remember that life is absurd, not a film, not a novel, and that you are constantly fighting against disorder and a lack of comprehension. Where there is no struggle, there is no strength.

I've heard that one somewhere ... Was that Kierkegaard? Sartre? Camus?

Oprah Winfrey, that one.

Enough, Guide, please, enough. This is absurd.

That's what I'm trying to tell you, Pilgrim! Life is absurd! Now fuck off and ride your bike!

Right: *Bagel? Check. Tube? Check. Gilet? Check. The Age of Reason? Check.*

Y is for Yarns

Sean Yates rode round Mallorca one morning for a laugh. Marco Pantani got down to 50kg by eating nothing but popcorn. Bernard Hinault won Liège–Bastogne–Liège by half an hour in a blizzard, and has had no feeling in the little finger of his left hand ever since. Eddy Merckx used to put steak in his shorts, ride a stage of the Tour de France on it and then hand it to the chef at that night's hotel to grill it up for his dinner. When Lance Armstrong crashed down on the crossbar in the Pyrénées that day, he was ironically the least likely man in the race to experience any pain in that area. Sean Kelly drove a journalist in search of an interview from Nice to Belgium and said only two words: hello and goodbye.

So what are you going to talk about on these long social rides that you've learned to perfect so effortlessly, Pilgrim? Don't say 'tell jokes'. Cyclists are rubbish at jokes. It's just not funny, cycling. Let me show you what I mean: a cyclist walks into a bar. Ouch.

Eh?

My point exactly. No jokes. However, a rich store of amusing and awe-inspiring cycling stories is a prerequisite. These will help while away the hours in a pleasant, entertaining yet educational manner. Ideally these stories will showcase the unremitting hardship that we tempered-steel characters endure on a minute-by-minute basis while adding a dash of humour and a soupçon of insanity. Let me give you a few to start you off. There are books full of this shit if it's your bag, and many are so well known that they're recited *en masse* like Monty Python's parrot sketch or Kip's Rex Kwon Do training session in *Napoleon Dynamite*. You know, the strength of a grizzly, the reflexes of a puma and the wisdom of a man.

Yes, I do know. You've mentioned it once or twice. In between your renditions of This is Spinal Tap *and* A Fistful of Travellers' Cheques.

I'm glad you've been listening, Pilgrim. Now, to make a good story, we're not talking about race results, though they can help sometimes. Strong characters tend to attract good stories, so many tales will gather around certain riders. Take Bernard Hinault. The last Frenchman to win the Tour was – sorry, is – an egomaniac of breathtaking proportions. His hilarious autobiography is full of openings along the lines of 'I woke up that morning and knew I would win'. The trouble is, unlike fantasists in the mould of Ian Poulter (I am the second-best golfer in the world) or Nicklas Bendtner (God cleans my football boots), Bernard Hinault (*le Blaireau*) could actually back up his posing with deeds. He dismissed Paris–Roubaix as a glorified cyclo-cross race, turned up, won it, then went home and never came back. He would ride on the front of the Tour de France peloton during his five victories turning a mahoosive gear around and staring out anybody that came up alongside him. But best of all stories revolving around Hinault was the 1980

Liège–Bastogne–Liège. The world's oldest, and some say hardest, bike race is held in the Ardennes at the end of April, so it's often lovely. In 1980, however, within minutes of the start, the riders found themselves in the middle of a heavy snowstorm. In shorts. As riders abandoned in their dozens, fighting to find a seat in a team car like musical chairs on ice, Hinault attacked, soloing away with one hand shielding his eyes from the blizzard. He rode the last painful 80km alone, increasing his advantage over the other survivors with every one, arriving in Liège nearly ten minutes ahead of anybody else. There were only twenty other finishers.

That's incredible. Was he all right?

Above: *L'Eroica. Those unsurfaced roads around Siena are a rich source of stories.*

Right: *I don't mind the shaggy dog stories, but please keep your shaggy dog under control.*

He says that he's never regained the full sensation in his left hand. Which is great really, because it feels like someone else is doing it, right?

I thought you said no jokes?

Good point. Hey, talking about things that aren't funny, have you ever seen the video of Lance slipping out of his pedals on Luz Ardiden in 2003? According to Morrissey, crashing down on the crossbar causes enough pain to make one shout for Buddha's respect. Ironic, then, that as far as we know, Lance had fewer testicles than any other of the centennial Tour de France's 198 starters. Still, taking into account the kind of day he was having, one crash already under his belt, I bet he still landed on the remaining *ballon d'or.*

Don't tell me: he went on to win the stage?

No, Pilgrim. How could he? Lance Armstrong doesn't exist, even if somebody bearing that name may indeed have crossed the line first that day. If you look at the results now, it says that the 2003 Tour de France had no winner, just like every other Tour between 1999 and 2006. Weird. Mind you, that's not even the winner of the Most Evocative Story About Bollock Pain In Cycling award. That must surely go to the greatest cyclist of all time, the man himself, Edouard Louis Joseph Merckx. He took his fifth and final Giro d'Italia victory in early June, which is when the race was held in those days, knocked off a quick Tour of Switzerland win for a laugh, then diverted his journey to the start of the Tour de France to have an operation on his perineum.

His biffin's bridge?

You really have been listening, haven't you, Pilgrim? Good lad. Anyway, by the time the Tour left Brest on

Left: *It was great in the olden days. No, really.*

the opening weekend, the operation scars had not only failed to clear up, they had opened up.

Jesus.

It is said that on that 1974 Tour win, the Cannibal's last, the chamois of his shorts was drenched in blood every night. Well might you pull that vom face, Pilgrim. One can only hope that by 1974 the world had moved on enough that Tour cyclists no longer laid a cut of sirloin in their gusset to soften the ride before asking the hotel chef to cook it up for them in the evening.

One bloody steak for table two, please.

Eddy Merckx won the Giro and Tour in the same season an unprecedented three times in his career. The last man to pull off the double was the late great Marco Pantani, another character to whom stories cling like barnacles. His victory on the sacred mountain of Oropa in the Piedmont Alps during the 1999 Giro is one of them. With 8km left to the summit finish, the shiny-headed maestro punctured. As race leader, he might have expected the 49-strong front group to wait for him, but they had obviously seen too many Italian footballers rolling around in apparent agony to want to kick the ball into touch voluntarily. Spitting mad, Pantani flew after them with his replaced wheel spinning faster than you can say 'Look out! Drugs raid!' and passed every single one of them before the top. That was quite a win, but he made a habit of victories like that. It's said that his obsessive need to be the world's greatest climber led him to drop his weight until he weighed less than 55kg. Eight and a half stone. He wasn't a tall man, but there aren't many five-foot-eight people who weigh less than that. And his secret, Pilgrim? Popcorn. Nothing else. He would ride his bike all day, come home and eat nothing but popcorn. I don't have the exact recipe, but one doubts it was Butterkist.

Do you think I should copy him, Guide?

Hmm. Pantani isn't really best placed to advise on how to be a Middle Aged Man In Lycra, seeing as how he didn't reach middle age. But if you want to be found dead of a cocaine overdose in a scuzzy hotel room at 34, go right ahead, son.

I think I prefer the stories you've been telling me about the Seans.

Yates and Kelly? Yeah, you can't beat them. Legends. And they retired just long enough ago – the nineties, both of them – that their respective exploits seem to gather mystique with every passing year. King Kelly, indisputably the greatest Irish cyclist until his contemporary Stephen Roche improbably brought home the Giro, Tour and Worlds all in one year, won more than any other rider in his heyday, and ranked world number one for nine years. But it's the stories about him off the bike that stick. You wouldn't guess it now that he's a broadcaster, but he just wouldn't talk to anyone. He would nod through radio interviews. He would fix would-be interlocutors with a stony stare that would reduce Jeremy Paxman to tears. One guy who came up with a ploy to get round his taciturn nature was a journalist who realised that Kelly would be driving home from the Riviera after Paris–Nice to his base in Belgium. The scribbler offered to pay for the petrol and struck the deal, confident that he would bring back a wonderfully in-depth profile of the great man. He reportedly got two words out of Kelly over the entire 1,200km: 'hello' and 'goodbye'.

He won more than Yates, then?

Oh yes, he was a different sort of rider. Yates was the most valued of *superdomestiques*, a rider who could do the work of a whole team but usually in the service of a more garlanded leader. An Englishman at the Tour when such a thing was a rarity, he was massively popular, but mainly for his feats of endurance rather than his results. Recovering in an Italian hospital after an operation on his foot, he decided to go for a ride to alleviate the boredom –

round Lake Como. Two hundred kilometres later, he was surprised to find a gaggle of panicking medics roundly castigating him on his return. Even more of these stories have come to light since his retirement. As Directeur Sportif in charge of the Astana team, he was spotted by the staff of other Giro d'Italia squads lying on the tarmac outside a convenience store during the rest day. He'd chosen to ride the 250km transfer between stages and was trying to revive himself with a bottle of mineral water. And nobody has ever gone on a trip to the cyclist's paradise of Mallorca and ridden the mountainous coast road to be told that Yates did a full circuit of the island on a training camp once: 330km in ten hours. It wasn't even his training camp: he was meant to be coaching people.

I suppose you could say he was leading by example.

I suppose. Example of what, I don't know. He does coaching for folks like you now, Pilgrim. You should give him a call. He supposedly had a short piece of advice for one of his charges who was unhappy with the severity of the training programme Yates had set him and was struggling to come to terms with its demands. Yates sent him a four-letter text saying 'HTFU'.

HTFU?

Harden the fuck up.

Cycling's full of yarns, eh?

There are just so, so many more. I could go on all night.

Yes, I have a feeling you could.

Left: *What? No, you HTFU.*

Z is for Zeitgeist

They say that cycling is the new golf. For one, they are both sports that cost as little or as much as you want. You can get your dad's old clubs or his steel Coventry Eagle tourer out of the garage and head out to the nearest municipal course or country lane. Or you can spend a fortune on Callaways and Pings or Pinarellos and Parlees and jet off to an exotic location.

Golf or cycling, there's every chance that your carefully packed equipment will either have disappeared or been sat on by Ganesh masquerading as an airport baggage handler by the time you're hanging around hopefully by the carousel.

Another thing the perfect swing and the perfect ride have in common is that they succeed through a process of putting a number of simple things together. Keep your head down, weight 60-40 on the balls of your feet, shirt tucked in, ridiculous coloured trousers, no mobile phones, no trainers, no socialists, nobody different in any way shape or form … we know it's hard to keep all those crucial points to the front of your mind when you're on the first tee. Especially when you're being obsequious to your smug boss and his smug boss. Applying the golf approach by breaking the whole caboodle down into manageable chunks, here is a handy checklist for the man in Lycra.

A is for Attitude
HTFU

B is for Bike
Never sacrifice style for speed

C is for Café
Life is too short to drink shit coffee

D is for Drugs
If it's available from the bar, it's allowed

E is for Etiquette
Don't be *that* guy

F is for Fit
The cheap bike that fits you will always beat the expensive one that doesn't

G is for Gears
You don't have to prove what a big man you are, but no triples

H is for Hills
There are no great flat bike rides

I is for Italiano
Some people have just got it, some are absolutely full of it

J is for Job
Stick to what you know and leave the rest to us

K is for Kit
There's no such thing as enough kit

L is for Legs
Don't be ashamed, be ashaved

M is for Mileage
There's no such thing as enough mileage

N is for No
If you have to ask, you know the answer

O is for Objectives
Be the best you can be

P is for Peloton
It's not all about you

Q is for Quackery
Only if the pros do it

R is for Racing
The single malt of bike riding

S is for Socks
If you can't get these right, give up

T is for Technology
They're handlebars, not computlebars

U is for Unlucky
When an unstoppable force meets an immovable object

V is for Vulcanised
You can't have a nice bike with shit wheels

W is for Winter
An opportunity to wear all of that nice stuff you bought

X is for Existentialism
Yes, it's stupid. Life is stupid. Ride your bike

Y is for Yarns
You can't beat a good story

Z is for Zeitgeist
It's meant to be fun

Right: *Job done. Thank you, Guide.*

Acknowledgements

Additional photography by John Deering, Dan Tsantilis and Emily Ashley.

Featuring James Wakelin as Pilgrim. We'd like to thank James
for his unending patience and enthusiasm.

This whole book would be a random mess of words and
pictures without Jane Ashley's consummate design skills.

Bob Johnson let us mess around with all his old crap. Again.

Thank you Giant Twickenham and Condor Cycles for your assistance.

Thanks to everybody who has ridden their bikes with us, drunk coffee
with us, eaten cake with us and listened to us rant along the way.